I0199119

LEGENDS,
LORE AND
SECRETS OF WESTERN
NEW YORK

LEGENDS, LORE AND SECRETS OF WESTERN NEW YORK

LORNA MACDONALD CZARNOTA

THE
History
PRESS

Published by The History Press
Charleston, SC 29403
www.historypress.net

Copyright © 2009 by Lorna MacDonald Czarnota
All rights reserved

First published 2009
Second printing 2010
Third printing 2012

ISBN 978-1-5402-2013-4

Library of Congress Cataloging-in-Publication Data
Czarnota, Lorna.
Legends, lore and secrets of Western New York / Lorna MacDonald Czarnota.
p. cm.
Includes bibliographical references.
ISBN 978-1-5402-2013-4
1. New York (State), Western--History. 2. Legends--New York (State), Western. 3.
Folklore--New York (State), Western. I. Title.
F126.9.C93 2009
398.209747--dc22
2009033677

Notice: The information in this book is true and complete to the best of our knowledge. It is offered without guarantee on the part of the author or The History Press. The author and The History Press disclaim all liability in connection with the use of this book.

All rights reserved. No part of this book may be reproduced or transmitted in any form whatsoever without prior written permission from the publisher except in the case of brief quotations embodied in critical articles and reviews.

I would like to dedicate this book to all of the residents of Western New York, past and present—to those who remain, those who have moved but wish they could be here and those whose footprints we can only hope to fill. Let us keep our courage and our brilliant diversity while looking forward to our children's legacy and continue to appreciate what has been given us.

CONTENTS

Acknowledgements   9
Introduction   11

An Ancient Seabed and an Ancient People   15
Forming a New Land   21
The War of 1812   45
Heart and Hardy   65
Giants in Western New York   99
Natural Wonders   115
Murder, Mayhem and More   123
Land of Spirits and the Burned-Over District   139

They Were Here: A Conclusion   149
Selected Bibliography   153
About the Author   155

ACKNOWLEDGEMENTS

The stories and information included in this book are built on many different sources and the hard work of others. I would like to acknowledge the many historical societies and museums across Western New York, in particular the librarians and historians at the Buffalo and Erie County Historical Museum; Mount Morris, Genesee and Livingston County Historical Societies; and the docents and historians at Old Fort Niagara. Also, thanks to all who have written and researched this region's history throughout the years. This book is a continuation of their efforts.

Special thanks to Rebecca Stone at Kill Buck Historical Society for information on the Whistling Well; Ossian town historian Rhea Walker for the Ossian Giant; and Livingston County's Amie Alden for Francis Bellamy, Mary Jemison and the Torture Tree. These ladies opened some history that was new to me, and I am grateful.

I would also like to thank my musician friends and band members Tom Naples and Jim Mumm, who gave me some valuable leads about Buffalo's rich musical history, and all the friends who have shared stories over the years, from the sea monster of Lake Erie to the strange story of William Morgan.

Thank you to The History Press for inviting me to write this book, to the hardworking editors and artists for their attention to detail and more than adequate communications to make this collection come to fruition.

Last but not least, I thank my friends and family, who allowed me the time and space needed to research and write. For several months they did not complain while I became a hermit, but I know that their support was what kept me going. Finally, a great big appreciation to Thomas Heim, who not only read my manuscript and helped with photographs but also, as a resident here from birth, is a daily reminder of what it means to be a Western New Yorker. His wealth of historical knowledge and patience are boundless.

INTRODUCTION

This book offers history, myths and legends from the counties that compose the region known as Western New York. Whenever possible, several versions of each story were compared and combined to give the reader the truest information and to remind him or her that stories change with various viewpoints. When not recorded in written form, they can be left to interpretation by whoever tells the tale. I wish readers to know that all stories in this book are as true as my research and resources allowed. Time and distance from events create myths that cannot always be proven. I am sorry that many other stories and variations could not be included. An area as expansive as Western New York, with as deep a history, could not be represented in one book, but that is the fun of writing about and exploring a region: constantly uncovering new and interesting facts and fictions.

Hundreds of books have been written about various events, eras, arts, architectures and prominent citizens of Western New York. I have attempted to bring under one cover those stories I considered most important to the formation of this region, as well as others that I felt were either very well known and deserved inclusion or lesser known and the reader would find them fascinating.

Since moving here in 1970, I have taken pride in calling myself a Buffalonian and Western New Yorker. I love the variety this area has to offer, with hills in the southern tier, two Great Lakes and many smaller ones, rivers and streams, the Erie Canal, forests and parks and enough historical sites to be enjoyed over the years. The richness of this region's history is deep and

A Holland Land Company map showing the counties of Western New York.

meaningful, tied to the formation of our country and that of our neighbors in Canada. We are inseparable.

The people living here have a unique spirit that I hope I have captured in this book. I am honored to tell their stories and am more aware than ever of how the landscape has shaped the residents and how they, in turn, have shaped the landscape. Western New Yorkers are strong-willed, stubborn, fun loving, kind and in love with their history. Coming from myriad cultures and backgrounds, they embody a special characteristic that sets them apart from the rest of New York State.

A Western New Yorker would rather forego the latest trends than tear down an old building if it has any kind of story or memory attached to it.

Sometimes it has been necessary to remove the old in favor of the new, but it is only done with a great deal of discussion and heart searching.

As I was writing this book, one of Buffalo's most memorable buildings was taken down near the waterfront to make way for harbor revitalization. When the wrecking ball struck Memorial Auditorium, families stood nearby, some with tears in their eyes, recalling the concerts, circuses and sporting events they had witnessed there. They took pictures, they told stories and they purchased what bits and pieces they could at auction, including seats and scoreboards. In today's throwaway society, I appreciate and respect that attitude.

Some may classify Western New York as "upstate," but it is as far removed in character as it is in distance from the rest of the state. It truly stands alone.

AN ANCIENT SEABED
AND AN ANCIENT PEOPLE

LAC DU CHAT

Lac du Chat, meaning "Lake of the Cat," was named by the French for its abundance of mountain lions and Eriez Indians, who wore clothing of cat hides and fur, trimmed with tails of the northern panther. The natives called the lake "Erie." The region surrounding the lake was a vast wooded wilderness. Only Indians and the occasional fur trader inhabited it until the French formally claimed, cleared and settled it.

Once an ancient lowland basin, the areas surrounding Lake Erie were rich in natural resources deposited by glaciers during the last ice age. Descendants of the fourteen-thousand-year-old glacial Lake Maumee, Lakes Erie and Ontario are two of the five Great Lakes composing the largest system of freshwater lakes in the world. As the shallowest, Lake Erie is the warmest and the most biologically productive. It forms New York State's western border, with Lake Ontario to the north.

Located above Niagara Falls, Lake Erie joins Lake Ontario via the Niagara River. Its location created a perfect avenue for early fur traders venturing north to Canada from Ohio, Pennsylvania and other points south. Portage trails allowed those wishing to travel both lakes to traverse the mighty Niagara, skirting the deadly falls.

Lake Erie is volatile and alive. A centerpiece for life in Western New York even today, the lake is noted for its recreational value and its ferocity. Storms crossing Lake Erie wreak havoc, especially in winter, bringing nationally famous blizzards and, in spring, creating ice floe backups on tributaries that erode the landscape. The residents here are as hardy now as they must have been in the region's earliest days.

No mountain lions live in the region today. Lac du Chat and the Eriez people are all but forgotten, but Western New York continues to be rough and tough. The city of Buffalo, at its center, is known as the "City of Good Neighbors."

THE CAT PEOPLE

The "Cat People," or Eriez Indians, lived along the southern shores of Lake Erie from Ohio to Western New York. Their name derives from *Erielhonan*, meaning "long tail," or *Erieehronan*, "people of the panther." Jesuit missionaries and the French, who eventually claimed the region, referred to them as the Nation du Chat. Their allies, the Hurons, called them *yeenresh*, "It is long tailed." The native population gave its name to the lake, the county surrounding Buffalo and the city of Erie, Pennsylvania, which was once one of their greater villages, "Rique."

Early accounts of the Cat People are limited to Jesuit writings of the mid-seventeenth century and word of mouth, mostly from the Huron. According to these accounts, white men had few encounters with the Eriez. Contact may have been limited to the Jesuits and perhaps Dutch fur traders from Fort Orange, now known as Albany. In 1615, Étienne Brûlé (the first European to see all of the Great Lakes) claimed to have met with a group of Eriez near Niagara Falls while pursuing his interest in the lifestyle of the Hurons. Regardless of these accounts, we still know little of their way of life, but we feel their presence.

A woodland nation, the Cat People kept to themselves, living off the fertile land. They were sedentary, living in pallisaded villages consisting of longhouses common to northeastern natives. Soil cultivation was familiar to the Eriez. Wild game was their mainstay in the winter months, but during the growing season they planted the Three Sisters: corn, beans and squash. These were among the earliest cultivated crops, perfect complements to one another. Corn is the pole on which the beans climb. The beans give back to the earth what the corn requires, making the corn stalks stronger. The squash roots act as mulch, shading weeds and keeping the rain in the ground.

LEGEND OF THE THREE SISTERS

As with many stories that were originally passed by word of mouth, the "Legend of the Three Sisters" can be found in many variants. All contain the sustaining plants of corn, beans and squash. All are tied in some way to creation myths. The following story is just one interpretation.

Sky Woman fell, landing on Turtle's back. When she landed, she gave birth to a daughter. This younger woman married West Wind, and she gave birth to twin sons. The sons fought each other before they were born, and their mother did not survive. Saddened by the loss of her daughter, Sky Woman buried her in the New Earth. From the grave grew three sacred plants, the Three Sisters.

The sisters, who lived together in a field, were different in their size and dress. The youngest wore green and at first could only crawl. The middle sister wore a bright yellow dress and was always running off by herself. The oldest sister was tall and always tried to protect her younger siblings. Yet for all their differences, the sisters loved one another dearly. Even the one who ran off never went far. Staying together made them strong.

Bean Sister climbed on Corn Sister. Squash Sister hugged the earth beneath them. Sky Woman's twin grandsons always had plenty to eat. All of humanity was nourished.

THE BEAVER WARS (1642–98)
AND THE EXTINCTION OF THE CAT PEOPLE

Fierce warriors, the Cat People (Eriez) were skilled hunters, using only bows and arrows reportedly tipped with poison. By the seventeenth century, a sudden surge in population increased the number of Cat People to well over fourteen thousand. At the same time, neighboring tribes and allies, such as the Hurons, had diminished from over twenty thousand to half that number due to European diseases and firearms.

As the Eriez grew stronger, the Hurons were getting weaker. The Eriez could be not trusted to keep the alliance between them, so when the French made firearms readily available through trade, the Hurons, Neutrals and Susquehannocks made sure that the Eriez did not obtain them. Simultaneously, the British armed the Iroquois, the Algonquins' traditional

Der Kürschner ("The Furriers"). Beaver pelts and other furs were sent to Europe from America. *Courtesy of the Library of Congress Prints and Photographs Division.*

enemy. Yet despite this disadvantage in weaponry, the Cat People held their own until near the end of the Beaver Wars.

The Eriez traded beaver pelts to the Susquehannocks for European goods at a very early date, but they were not the only ones who wanted pelts. Their rivals on all sides, including the Iroquois, traded pelts for guns and metal tools. As these beaver pelts became scarcer, the Eriez encroached on neighboring territories to get them.

In 1635, a war ensued between the Cat People and their neighbors. The Eriez and their allies withdrew support from a third group, the Wenro, who were left vulnerable to attack from the Iroquois. A traditional hatred between the Eriez allies and the Iroquois snowballed into the Beaver Wars in 1642.

The Iroquois defeated the Hurons, who fled to take shelter with the Eriez. The Eriez refused to hand these refugees over to their enemies. This struggle continued for two years, even as other tribes in the Iroquois Confederation began warring with the Susquehannocks. Although several unsuccessful attempts at peace were made, the seriously damaged Eriez alliances were finally broken.

THE STRAW THAT BROKE THE CAT'S BACK

On one occasion, perhaps the last time the Eriez would consider a treaty, the Cat Nation sent thirty representatives to a conference with the Senecas. During the meeting, a fight broke out and one of the Eriez killed a Seneca. Iroquois law said that a life taken was to be punished by a life given. As a result, all but five ambassadors were slain.

The final days of war between the Iroquois and the Eriez began. In retaliation, the Eriez attacked, burned a Seneca village and then intercepted a scouting party, capturing one of their sachem, Annenrae, in 1653.

Champlain Exploring the Canadian Wilderness. Courtesy of the Library of Congress Prints and Photographs Division.

Legend says that, according to custom, the Cat People planned to have Chief Annenrae adopted by the sister of one of the fallen ambassadors. She was away, and they did not wish to waste time, so they prepared for the ceremony. The Eriez leaders were surprised when, upon her return, the fallen ambassador's sister refused Annenrae. Instead, she wished him to die in revenge for her brother. He was burned at the stake.

The Senecas attacked Rique (now Erie, Pennsylvania) in 1654. Although the Cat People made a valiant attempt to defend their village, they were soon overpowered and the village burned. It is said that fires lit the sky as every man, woman and child was put to death by burning . The people known as Nation du Chat came to an end.

Not all the Cat People died in the Beaver Wars, but they would never have the strength to continue as a united people. Many were eventually assimilated into the Seneca culture. Today, many Senecas can trace their lineage to the Eriez, the people who wore cat tails.

FORMING A NEW LAND

THE GHOST SHIP OF THE GREAT LAKES

Robert Cavelier, Sieur de La Salle, spent his childhood and early years as a young man restless and frustrated. He became a Jesuit novice, but that sedentary life did not suit him. Always at odds with superiors and unwilling to conform, Robert left the priesthood for New France in 1665. He took up fur trading near Montreal. A land grant at the juncture of the St. Lawrence River and Lake Ontario helped La Salle create a monopoly on fur trade, making him a very wealthy man.

Fur trading brought La Salle into relations with the Indians. He was fascinated by their stories of a great river that flowed westward. He thought this might have been a passage to China, something he dreamed of finding for many years. Always a dreamer and schemer, with access to some of the most important waterways in North America, La Salle returned to France for permission to start western colonies as he explored. When he returned to New France, Robert sold everything and set off in search of the river. Accompanying him were his lieutenant, La Motte, and a priest named Father Hennepin.

Traveling on Indian trails in December 1687, Father Hennepin went ahead of the main party and became the first European to come face to face with one of the world's natural wonders. The Niagara's roar must have been deafening as he gazed at the mist above the falls, which held a spiritual quality that the Indians celebrated long before this French priest

Avantures mal-heureuses du Sieur de la Salle. Courtesy of the Library of Congress Prints and Photographs Division.

arrived. Father Hennepin made the first account and sketch of the falls, which appeared in his 1699 book *New Discovery*. La Salle soon stood beside the priest, looking on in wonder.

In January 1679, the explorers climbed the Niagara escarpment on Indian portage trails. Upstream about two miles, La Salle began planning a fleet that would carry men, supplies and furs between trading posts on the Great Lakes and the western colonies of his dreams.

La Salle's *Griffon* was the first ship to sail the Great Lakes. A marvel among the natives, who were amazed that white men could build such a vessel of wood, the ship was sixty feet high, with a griffin on the prow. The griffin, a symbol of vigilance and strength, was the crest of their benefactor, Compte de Frontenac.

Building began above Niagara Falls. The party towed the ship to Squaw Island at present-day Buffalo, New York. A five-man crew, along with the three explorers, set sail in August. They landed at Green Bay, Wisconsin, where the *Griffon* was loaded with furs to pay La Salles' debtors. Hennepin, La Salle and La Motte remained in Wisconsin to continue their explorations, while the five-man crew returned east toward the Niagara.

The loss of the *Griffon* is one of sailing history's most profound mysteries. It, along with its crew, was lost, never to return. Many believe it is at the bottom of Lake Michigan or Huron. For over three hundred years, it has haunted the dreams of the curious. Of one thing we can be certain, the *Griffon* is somewhere, with all its cargo and the bones of those who sailed it, perhaps not as strong but surely vigilant. The "Ghost Ship of the Great Lakes," built in Western New York, was the first commercial vessel lost on the lakes but not the last. It now watches over more than six thousand other ships that have joined it in that watery grave.

THE FRENCH AND INDIAN WAR (1689 1763)

The Beaver Wars morphed into the dispute between the British and the French over the New World. The French and Indian conflict is the last of these events, encompassing the Beaver Wars and King George's War (1744–48).

The Iroquois, led by the Mohawks, wanted to expand their territories, cornering fur trade with the Europeans. One result of this bloody conflict was the destruction of many Great Lakes tribes—the Hurons, Eriez, Neutrals and Susquehannocks. Survivors fled west of the Mississippi, transplanting native tribes such as the Lakotas, who then moved to the western plains. When refugees returned many years later, they could no longer organize into single ethnic communities. The Iroquois also lost their alliance with the Dutch and were pawns in an age-old game between the English and their enemy, the French.

Too Near the War Path. Settlers braved the wilderness, always knowing that danger lurked nearby. *Courtesy of the Library of Congress Prints and Photographs Division.*

Forming a New Land

The first Europeans to encounter the Iroquois were the French, as early as the 1540s, when Jacques Cartier, who claimed Canada for France, met them on the St. Lawrence River. Wars between the Iroquois and the Algonquin peoples of the Great Lakes region already had a long history by this time. In the early seventeenth century, Samuel de Champlain, allied to the Hurons, battled with the Iroquois on the shores of Lake Champlain. He killed two Iroquois chiefs with firearms, something new to the natives. As a result, the Iroquois had no love for the French.

By the 1630s, the Iroquois had traded enough furs with the Dutch to have an ample supply of firearms. Beaver populations dwindled because they were so highly sought after as the main currency for trade. The Iroquois, like the Eriez, encroached on hunting territories. The Iroquois' desire to be the "middlemen" in the fur trade grew. At the same time, professional French soldiers arrived in Canada in the late 1660s. The Dutch lost control of their southern colony to the British. England claimed lands west of the Appalachians to the Mississippi by royal grants. France claimed the St. Lawrence River territory and the Mississippi River watershed via explorations by Robert de La Salle. The native populations claimed the lands by birth and blood. Everybody wanted to control the same place at the same time.

The stage was set for the French and Indian War, with Western New York outside the "Western Door" of the Iroquois Confederation longhouse, the door guarded by the Senecas. Western New York found itself squeezed between the French and Hurons on one side and the British and Iroquois on the other.

Although Western New York was not the main front for this war, as it had been during the Beaver Wars, it played a crucial role as a pathway west via Lake Ontario, the Niagara River and Lake Erie. The French found it necessary to fortify the region with a fort at the mouth of the river near Youngstown. All boats entering the Niagara passed beneath its guns. Whoever controlled the fort controlled passage to the interior of North America.

Fort Niagara

Robert de La Salle originally founded Fort Niagara in 1679 on what had first been the Neuter Indian tribe's territory and later Seneca land. La Salle used the site as a supply base while building his ship, the *Griffon*. He called the fortification Fort Conti. The Iroquois destroyed the structure after it was

Fort Niagara, French and Indian War reenactment. *Courtesy of the author.*

abandoned. A new fort was built in 1687 by the Marquis de Devonville, governor of New France. This fort was equally doomed to destruction.

After French and Indian relations improved in 1725, the French were given permission to build a new structure. "French Castle" was a stone building, appearing as little more than a trading post and used as such for a brief time. Although it was not called French Castle until the 1800s, this is the oldest building currently on the site.

THE GHOST OF FRENCH CASTLE

Old Fort Niagara's history is one of bloodshed and destruction, with death and fire leaving scars that cannot always be seen.

The French Castle is a beautiful building of area stone and wooden beams. On the main floor is a well. Most fortifications had a well so that man and beast could be watered without venturing outside. But this well is haunted, or so legend says. Since 1839, many people have reported seeing a headless ghost.

According to legend, two officers of the garrison fell in love with a native woman from a nearby village. The castle's first level was a trading post, and many Indians came there to trade. She was probably someone's daughter. This wilderness was no place for European women, so surely the "pickings" were few, or perhaps this young woman's beauty was unsurpassed.

One night, as the two officers played cards, talked, drank or all three, they happened to mention this beautiful native woman. Soon, it became apparent that they spoke of the same woman. Most likely they had been drinking because one thing led to another and swords were drawn. In the end, one officer lost his head.

It must have been quite a job cleaning up after the murder while making sure nobody heard the commotion. The killer dragged the body to the well and hefted it in with a splash. He secreted the head through the sally port. A second splash sent the head into the river.

On nights when the moon is full, they say the body rises from the well and searches for its head.

ROBERT ROGERS: RANGER AND SCOUT

The second floor of French Castle housed a chapel said to have been Western New York's earliest permanent church. A narrow room at the end of the corridor was used briefly as a cell for Robert Rogers in 1768.

Born to Irish immigrant parents, Rogers grew up on the New Hampshire frontier. As a young man, he served as a scout in King George's War. Then, in 1758, Rogers was given command of all rangers. It was Rogers and his rangers whom the British sent when taking possession of the French Great Lakes posts in 1760.

Rogers was a hero in war but a bit of a scoundrel during peacetime. His involvement in British New World war efforts was a result of an official pardon for his actions as a counterfeiter. If war hadn't broken out, he most likely would have been thrown into prison. The Seven Years' War was his savior, at least temporarily.

Rogers married in 1760, shortly after the rangers were disbanded, but he was a restless spirit and took command of mercenaries in 1761. His role was to pacify the Cherokees in North Carolina. Even with all this, Rogers's efforts and hard work serving king and country proved meaningless and his pay was cut in half following the French and Indian War. Eventually, Rogers returned to England and wrote a couple of books and plays. Along the way, Rogers made a powerful enemy in General Thomas Gage.

Rogers, a frontier "bad boy," did things his own way. His guerilla military tactics earned him hero status, but his later dealings with the Indians did not please the British, nor was Gage thrilled with the friendship Rogers built with his rival, General Amherst. Gage put spies on Rogers's activities, intercepting his mail and questioning Rogers's subordinates, including a private secretary. According to the secretary Rogers had angered, Rogers said he would offer his services to the French if the British didn't take his advice on governance. General Gage finally found the chink in Rogers's armor that he'd been looking for. Furthermore, Rogers was accused of illicit trade with the Indians. He was arrested and charged with treason. He was sent to Montreal in chains to stand trial. That journey, in 1767, took him through Western New York, with a layover in a Fort Niagara cell.

Ever a somewhat lucky man, Rogers was defended by his friend General Amherst and acquitted. He went back to England to ask forgiveness of financial debts, but his luck ran out. King George was fed up with him and sent Rogers to debtor's prison. Later, Robert Rogers would be best known for his desire to find the Northwest Passage.

THE SURRENDER OF FORT NIAGARA
(JULY 14–25, 1759)

In the early days of the French and Indian conflicts, the Iroquois attempted to remain neutral. When they did take sides, they chose whoever would meet their needs. Just prior to the battle for Fort Niagara, the Iroquois sided with the French. They switched rapidly when it became obvious that the English had more to offer. This was largely due to an Irish colonist, Sir William Johnson. After the death of his first wife, Sir William married the sister of Mohawk chief Joseph Brant.

William Johnson was just twenty-three years of age when his uncle asked him to oversee lands he had been granted in the New World. A portion of these lands in the Mohawk Valley were to be his own. Sir William built a home in what is now called Johnstown and, by order of the Crown, befriended the Mohawk Indians. They accepted him as a chief among them. Johnson adopted their language and their manner of dress. Ever a shrewd businessman, he supplied traders and bought their furs to cut out middlemen who previously dealt with Albany. The Indians were also welcome at his home, Mount Johnson. Many conferences were held there.

When war ensued, fearing that the French would enlist the Hurons, Johnson convinced the Mohawks to side with Britain.

Johnson's methods of engaging the Indians were less than humane, earning him an amount of infamy. He turned a blind eye to brutality when the natives scalped and burned the settlers and destroyed their homes. Johnson paid a bounty for scalps. Knowing that he could not control who would be scalped, he put a lower price on the scalps of children. His tactics are disputed in some accounts.

Without modern mass communications, the Indians' switch in sides did not reach all the Iroquois. In fact, when the British marched on Fort Niagara with their Iroquois allies, there were thirty Senecas still within the fort, siding with the French. Fortunately for the French, Captain Pierre Pouchot decided to send the Senecas out to their Iroquois brothers rather than risk them turning on his forces during the attack.

The battle in which the British gained Fort Niagara, ultimately winning the war for them, was really one of those instances when fate played a role.

Captain Pouchot had three thousand men in his command at the fort. In a foolhardy decision, he sent over two thousand of those men to fight against British-held Fort Pitt (Fort Duquesne). This left only five hundred soldiers and thirty Senecas to defend Fort Niagara, but he had no way of knowing that the days ahead would doom his command.

The British force arriving to attack in July 1759 consisted of two thousand soldiers and one thousand Iroquois. William Johnson was among them, under command of Brigadier General John Prideaux. When the general was killed in battle, Johnson took command. His alliance with the Iroquois would prove useful, although the Indians did not fight for or against either side at the fort proper. Always wishing to remain neutral, they chose to retreat to the woods of La Belle Famille, leaving the Europeans to kill one another.

Pouchot sent south for reinforcements. On July 20, the French in the fort saw these reinforcements on the Niagara River. Approximately sixteen hundred soldiers and native allies canoed along Lake Erie, portaged the falls and came to the rescue. The French commander was unaware that British scouts had also seen them. Johnson prepared a welcome, and Pouchet's reinforcements never arrived at the fort.

LA BELLE FAMILLE MASSACRE

"The Beautiful Family," a wooded area one mile south of Fort Niagara, has an onerous history that hardly suits its name. Jesuits traveling the region in the seventeenth century may have built a small shrine there, explaining the name. If so, the memory is lost and nothing remains of it.

The Battle of La Belle Famille is one of those moments in history when the tables are turned, when the opposition used its enemy's tactics against it. Throughout the French and Indian War, the French typically used Indian ambushes against the British. At La Belle Famille in 1759, the British laid the ambush. It is considered one of the bloodiest battles of the war.

Johnson acted quickly when scouts reported French reinforcements. He sent some of his Indians to intercept natives traveling with them. Johnson also dispatched about 150 soldiers under the command of Captain James de Lancey to block the road with a log breastwork. Johnson's Iroquois warriors, numbering 500, took positions in the woods on either side of the road at La Belle Famille.

De Lancey's fortifications were sound, but he decided that he needed a cannon. On July 24, he ordered some of his men to cross the river to get one, the closest available cannon in his estimation. Those soldiers never got to the water's edge, nor did they return. As they reached sight of the river, they were suddenly attacked by French Indian scouts and captured or killed. Those who were killed were scalped, and their heads were impaled on poles. The place of their massacre is now known as "Bloody Run."

Spurred into action upon hearing the gunfire and screams, de Lancey sent for support troops engaged at the fort. In the meantime, the French, following on the heels of their scouts, closed the gap. British allied Iroquois still waited silently in the woods.

The blocked roadway was easily seen. As the French neared, two Iroquois approached. In their native tongue, they asked the Indians allied to the French to step aside. All but thirty did so, leaving the French with only 350 soldiers and 100 New York militiamen. Even so, the French felt certain that they could continue with their plan because their captives confessed that only 150 British soldiers lay hidden behind the breastworks. What they did not know was that de Lancey had increased that number to nearly 500.

La Belle Famille site marker. Once a bloody battlefield, this woodland is now a residential neighborhood filled with shadows of the past. *Courtesy of the author.*

The confident French charged the British blockade and were easily pushed back. In a matter of ten minutes, some 250 men fell.

Some accounts claim that the French commander was wounded and his forces were given quarter and permission to leave peacefully. The French, knowing they could not move forward, retreated at a run. Patiently waiting until the French fled, the Iroquois rushed from the woods, killing and capturing many more in a six-mile pursuit.

As with many stories, facts are blurred by time. Reports are mixed about the treatment of the captured and fleeing Frenchmen. Some say that many scalps were taken, but humanely, if such a thing can be done. Others say that the Iroquois butchered with tomahawks and long knives and that Johnson, having struck a secret bargain with them, allowed the Indians to take prisoners for the purpose of adoption and sacrifice by burning.

Rules of war and laws for living were different for the Indians. They believed in a life for a life, including adoption as a means to replace slain family members.

While we may not be able to know the truth about the treatment of these captives, we can say that blood spilled on that terrible day at La Belle Famille.

Because reinforcements did not arrive at the fort, the French could not hold out against superior British force. The fort was sandwiched between the earthwork siege on land and British guns across the river. With the fort torn to shreds and French soldiers afraid to poke their heads out for repairs, it eventually fell. Pouchot surrendered the following day, July 25. He was taken alive and sentenced to imprisonment.

The British not only won a fort but also blocked the west so that no support reached French strongholds. Because Pouchot had to recall his army from its march to Fort Pitt, the British kept control of that fort as well.

The French and Indian War all but ended in September of that year when the British took the fort in Quebec. Once more, the Niagara River and Western New York played key roles in history. Unfortunately, winning Fort Niagara did not prove beneficial to the Iroquois. It actually forced them into a dependency with Britain, which served the colonists, not the Indians. Their way of life would never be the same. William Johnson died suddenly in 1774 during a heated conference with natives at his home.

THE MAID OF THE MIST

The first people to settle the Niagara Peninsula arrived from southwestern Ontario about AD 1400. One of the earliest native tribes called itself the Ongiaras, giving the river its name. Later tribes came to be known as the Neutrals or Neuters, a name given to them by French explorers because they acted as peacekeepers between the Hurons and Iroquois. The Neutrals were all but annihilated during the Beaver Wars. Since that time, the Senecas have called Niagara their home.

Water draws people to it, and people draw their lives from water. The mighty Niagara River and cataracts not only have significant histories but also spiritual power for those who live nearby. The following is a Seneca legend that shows their reverence for this place.

For many years, the natives lived alongside the Niagara. They drank from and fished in its waters. The thundering falls were present in their every waking hour and most likely in their dreams. It was the domain of the Thunder God Hinum and his two sons, who lived behind the falls.

One day, things changed dramatically for the Indians. Many fell ill with some strange sickness. They died one after the other. Stranger still was the fact that those who were buried were unearthed and devoured. The medicine men could find no cause for these events.

"We have done something to displease Hinum. We must make a sacrifice to appease him."

They filled a birch bark canoe with fruits and sent it over the roaring falls, where it vanished in the mists. They believed that the sacrifice would solve their woes, but it did not. The Indians decided to make a yearly sacrifice of one maiden. Perhaps that would appease the Thunder God. Still, they grew sick and died, or else their hunting failed or other inexplicable events caused them concern.

In 1679, when La Salle was exploring the Niagara, it was decided that the chief's own daughter, Lelawala, would give her life to benefit her people. La Salle protested, but the natives would not listen, and if her father was unhappy, it did not show on his face. They placed her in the white canoe and surrounded her with fruits and other gifts of the earth. All watched as the canoe dipped out of sight over the cataract.

Lelawala fell; the canoe flipped end over end, scattering gifts into the mist around her. Suddenly, the maiden felt herself land as strong, muscular arms interrupted her fall. One of Hinum's sons held her safely. She was rescued, but only if she would agree to marry him. Lelawala, mindful of why her people had sacrificed her, agreed on one condition.

"My people are dying and their graves are desecrated. I will marry you if you will help them."

"Very well," said the young god. "Your people are being stalked by the great snake that lives in the river. It poisons your water. When people are buried, it comes in the night and eats them."

Lelawala asked to return to her people to tell them of the snake.

"Tell them they must drink only from the streams," he said. "When the great snake comes, they must kill him with their spears."

In spirit form, the maiden told her people what to do. At first, the snake was only wounded, but it was a mortal wound. He crawled to the edge of the

Niagara Falls from Prospect Point. *Courtesy of the Library of Congress Prints and Photographs Division.*

falls. His head became wedged between two rocks on one side of the river and his tail between rocks on the other side. Writhing in his death thralls, the snake curled. That is how the Horseshoe Falls of Niagara took shape.

Other versions of this story say that as Lelawala's father saw her canoe near the edge, he leapt into a canoe to save her. Both canoes fell, and only the girl was saved. It makes sense to us that a father would rescue his child, but perhaps it also makes sense that the chief would not because his people's needs came first. Whichever version is told, it is a lovely story that truly expresses the power of the river and the Indians' spiritual connection to it.

BEAU FLEUVE AND NEW AMSTERDAM

A vast basswood forest once clouded the landscape to the shores of Lake Erie. Inhabited by the Kahkwas Indians, members of the Iroquois Nation, this region—"the Land of Basswoods"—included what would become the second-largest city in New York State. Sieur de La Salle sailed his ship, the *Griffon*, here from the river in 1679, and the first European settler in the region, a French fur trader, opened a trading post in 1758. Beau Fleuve has a humble but significant past and has been called by many names.

The naming of the city of Buffalo remains a mystery. Some say it was Father Hennepin, first to gaze upon Niagara Falls, who exclaimed "Beautiful River!" translated in French as *Beau Fleuve*.

The Kahkwas were supplanted by the Senecas in 1780, when the Senecas were driven west during the Sullivan Campaign, a Revolutionary War reprisal to break the Iroquois Confederacy that sided with Britain. The Senecas settled near an inland creek. One theory about the name comes from an account by a captive English family published in 1784. They stated that they heard Indians calling the creek "Buffalo," which may have been a misinterpretation of Beaver Creek, since the native word for beaver and buffalo are similar. Later that year, the treaty signed at Fort Stanwix in Rome, New York, listed the name of the Indian settlement as "the village on the Buffalo," later shortened to Buffalo Village.

The British took control of the region from the French following the French and Indian War. In 1792, after the Revolution, the Holland Land Company purchased it. By 1798, there were already a few houses built in the village. The Holland Land Company commissioned surveyor Joseph Ellicott, who had assisted his brother Andrew in designing Washington, D.C., to create the same hub design for this new city. The first lots were sold in 1804. Ellicott proposed the Dutch name New Amsterdam, but people living there preferred Buffalo (the anglicized "Beau Fleuve") or Buffalo Creek. Settlers disregarded Ellicott's city name, street names and designs for Main Street. The town was incorporated in 1810.

No buffalo have ever been substantiated in the region, although early French reports spoke of buffalo on Lake Erie's southern shore. It is more likely that Indians called it Beaver Creek in honor of the abundance of beaver important to their trade. Other names that did not survive include the early native name "the Land of Basswoods" and the French "River of Horses."

Buffalos, beavers and beautiful rivers are nothing alike, yet the people here are as industrious as the beaver, as beautiful as the river and as stubborn and strong-willed as the buffalo, so any of these names do them justice. Whatever they call their city, they always call it home.

REBELLION (1775–83)

As in the French and Indian War, Western New York was not the main theatre for the Revolutionary War, or, if you were a Loyalist, "the rebellion against the Crown." Yet it did play a role that changed the face of New York State. Painting a picture of life here at that time requires a historical view of events leading up to 1776, when the colonists declared their independence.

The first explorers literally bumped into this New World while searching for a more direct route to India and China. Little by little, aristocrats peopled the eastern seaboard with land grants from the British Crown, slaves, indentured servants and criminals seeking to avoid prison. The Dutch, Spanish and French explored different sectors of this land in a race for worldwide expansion.

Western New York remained a wilderness frontier until many years after His Majesty's thirteen colonies were established. As late as 1773, New York State west of Albany was largely uncharted, with only a few stouthearted colonists settling along the Mohawk River. As time passed, the valley became dotted with fortified homesteads such as Fort Klock.

However, Western New York was as far away for the colonists as Europe might seem to us today. The French were first to arrive here, coming south from Canada and north from Louisiana to expand their lands and fur trade. With this expansion came the need for forts to protect these new lands. The French established Fort Niagara and lost it to Britain during the French and Indian War. The British continued manning the fort and improving on its construction. This fort was about the only thing in Western New York with any substance at that time. Even when war broke out against the British with the first shots at Lexington and Concord, it is doubtful that the handful of settlers on the Niagara frontier knew anything about it for some time. Even then, it must have felt like war was someplace else, far away in someone else's backyard.

Regardless, Western New York would become a staging ground for some of the most brutal raids against colonists in the Mohawk Valley and

The Pioneer. Rugged outdoorsmen, traders and trappers roamed the wilderness freely, trading not only their goods but also stories of their adventures. *Courtesy of the Library of Congress Prints and Photographs Division.*

elsewhere. Indians living in New York State, coerced into fighting for one side or the other, were eventually pushed farther west from their lands, until the Senecas were forced to make this region their new homeland.

BUTLER'S RANGERS

The Revolutionary War, called by some "America's first Civil War," pitted neighbor against neighbor and brother against brother. Until that time, most of the colonists were considered British citizens, liable to laws of the Crown of England. Many remained so, while others chose to rebel. It is hard to imagine how this might have affected people living then. It must have been difficult to have such heartfelt desires to be free of tyranny when those living next to you were Loyalists. Your sedition could cost you your home or lead to imprisonment or death.

One Loyalist whose tactics and involvement made his name a rallying cry for Patriots was John Butler. Both he and Sir William Johnson became Canadian heroes but remained villains in American Patriot eyes.

John Butler was born in Connecticut. Just after his birth in 1728, his father, who was an officer in the king's army, left for the Mohawk Valley and a post at Fort Hunter. (This landmark was later demolished to make way for the Erie Canal.)

After acquiring land across the river from the fort, John's father sent for the family. John, the youngest son, was fourteen years old. Later, following in his older brothers' footsteps, John Butler took service with William Johnson's Department of the Six Nations during the French and Indian War. He led Indians under William Johnson in the attack against Fort Niagara in 1759. Successful, Butler married the wealthy daughter of a Dutch family residing in the valley, and together they raised a family.

During the peace that followed the war, Butler managed his own estate of twenty-six thousand acres. He and Johnson's Department of Indians moved to Montreal at the beginning of the Revolutionary War. In November 1775, Butler and his older son, Walter, were sent to Niagara to manage Indian affairs. Butler's name became despised throughout the valley. Rebels held his wife and other children prisoners until 1780.

Butler, in support of William's son John Johnson, led a large party of Indians in August 1777 against rebel forces at the Battle of Oriskany. Successful, Butler was given authorization to form what came to be known

The Wyoming Massacre. *Courtesy of the Library of Congress Prints and Photographs Division.*

as Butler's Rangers. Headquartered at Fort Niagara, his corps of rangers grew to ten companies, which fought in every major battle on the northern frontier. At one time, there were over nine hundred men in service.

Butler's Rangers' main directive was to harass and attack frontier settlements known to side with or give aid to rebel forces and to clear the way for the British to accomplish their task of defeating the rebellion. From their base at Fort Niagara, John led his rangers and Indians in the Wyoming Massacre at Forty Fort in Pennsylvania, killing hundreds of men, women and children. His forces moved northward again to attack settlers on the New York frontier, including German Flatts settlements in the Mohawk Valley. They returned to Fort Niagara with almost three hundred scalps taken in Pennsylvania.

In late 1778, John's son Walter led rangers and Indians at the Cherry Valley Massacre, where they slew thirty settlers indiscriminately. Accounts give various reasons for their actions, from retribution for burning Tioga to broken promises that defeated rebels would lay down arms, not to fight again.

Regardless, innocent men, women and children died under the tomahawk, including some who were loyal to England.

It is important to note that John Butler was not alone in the raids from Fort Niagara. John Johnson, as well as Sayenqueraghta, Cornplanter and Joseph Brant, some of the most significant native chiefs among the Senecas and Mohawks, joined Butler in the more important raids.

The final ranger company was disbanded in 1784. With land grants from the Crown, many rangers settled in Niagara, Canada, creating a Loyalist base that proved useful during the War of 1812. A war hero on the losing side, John Butler took up his old way of life as a farmer in Niagara. Others, including the Brants, joined him.

Today, a section of the Canadian army, the Lincoln and Welland Regiment in St. Catharine's Ontario (just thirty miles from Buffalo), is the military descendant of Butler's Rangers.

Atrocities at Forty Fort and Cherry Valley left harsh memories, but a bridge named "the Peace Bridge" and a long history of friendship span the Niagara River today, connecting Western New York and Canada. We look across the river, knowing that we share the same roots.

SULLIVAN'S CAMPAIGN AND THE NEW LANDSCAPE

General George Washington found it difficult to spare regular troops to protect the frontier. Instead, settlers relied on local militia to fend off attacks. Following the Wyoming and Cherry Valley Massacres, it became evident that a more aggressive strategy was needed. When the British turned their efforts toward colonies in the South in 1779, Washington saw an opportunity to launch an offensive into New York, intending to capture Fort Niagara. The campaign was offered to Horatio Gates, who had secured victory at Saratoga, but he refused. Instead, Washington turned to General John Sullivan:

> *The Expedition you are appointed to command is to be directed against the hostile tribes of the Six Nations of Indians, with their associates and adherents. The immediate objects are the total destruction and devastation of their settlements, and the capture of as many prisoners of every age and sex as possible. It will be essential to ruin their crops now in the ground and prevent their planting more.*

Washington's orders continue, but this excerpt is chilling enough. Sullivan was to leave a deliberate wake of destruction across New York's frontier as he moved westward toward the Niagara. Unfortunately for the Indians, their British allies gave them little help. When they did, it was too late.

The first native village to fall was the main Onondaga village west of Fort Stanwix. Continental soldiers killed twelve and took thirty-three prisoners, mostly neutrals, women and children. Colonel Van Schaik carried out this directive while Sullivan was ordered to march to the Susquehanna in central Pennsylvania. Sullivan then followed the river to Tioga, near current-day Athens, Pennsylvania. A compatriot, General James Clinton carried out his orders westward along the Mohawk River and then traveled to meet Sullivan at Tioga. This three-pronged sweep using Oneida scouts left forty Iroquois villages destroyed, along with their crops. Little could stop the devastation as the Continental army moved like locusts across the landscape. British-

The Torture Tree in Cuylersville. Sullivan's officers Boyd and Parker were tortured on this tree in one of the Senecas' largest villages. Little Beard's Town was destroyed. This was the farthest west the Revolutionary War would reach. *Courtesy of the author.*

loyal natives who were not engaged elsewhere fled before them. Sullivan and Clinton met only one real obstacle at the Newton battle near Elmira, New York. Here, they defeated Loyalists and Indians under command of John Butler and Joseph Brant.

A fourth attachment followed the Allegheny River from Fort Pitt with Colonel Daniel Brodhead in command. It crossed the southern border of Western New York. With most native warriors defending their homeland by facing General Sullivan, Brodhead met little resistance. He decimated ten villages, including Conewango, as he continued the planned march to meet Sullivan at the Seneca village of Geneseo for an attack on Fort Niagara. However, Brodhead only went as far as a village near modern-day Salamanca; he destroyed it and then turned back. The campaign ended when Clinton reached Ticonderoga. Sullivan's campaign was halted due to the lack of supplies, but enough damage was done. To this day, the Iroquois name for General George Washington is "Town Destroyer."

More than five thousand Iroquois refugees struggled through that winter, both in- and outside the wall of Fort Niagara. Though many had been sickened before the campaign, the wasting of their homes and crops contributed greatly to their demise. Starvation and bitter cold ended the lives of the weakest among them.

To punish the Oneidas for their role in Sullivan's campaign, Joseph Brant continued to lead attacks against Oneida villages. One unintended consequence of the American Revolution was an Indian civil war that killed many on both sides.

Throughout the Revolutionary War, the Tuscarora and Oneida tribes of the Iroquois Confederacy had managed to remain neutral or helpful to the Patriots. Near the end, however, many changed sides to aid the British because they saw their possible destruction.

Sullivan's campaign failed to capture Fort Niagara, and General Philip Schuyler, who had helped prepare defenses for the battle at Saratoga, attempted to send allied Indians to Fort Niagara to treat with the British allied Iroquois. It is no real surprise that, suspicious of a trick, they refused. Trust had been broken, and Sullivan retired his commission shortly thereafter.

Devastating as Sullivan's campaign had been to their homeland, native warriors continued to menace the frontier throughout the remainder of the war. It was women, children and the elderly who suffered most. The most stunning example of this is found in the story of Mary Jemison, the white woman taken prisoner, sold and adopted by two Iroquois women who lost their brother in warfare. Mary was considered a sister to them.

The burial site of Mary Jemison at Letchworth State Park. William Pryor Letchworth erected this statue commemorating the "White Women of the Genesee," who lived and is buried in the place she loved. Mary died at Buffalo Creek in 1833. *Courtesy of the author.*

Fleeing Sullivan's troops with her children, Mary lived a short time in Little Beard's Town before settling at Buffalo Creek, where she died at age ninety. The story of her life among the Indians is compelling. She witnessed things that most of us cannot even imagine.

The Iroquois Confederacy was irreparably broken; its standard of life was gone. Native lands were secured in the Treaty of Fort Stanwix but lost again in a controversial treaty with New York State. The nations that had been pushed into the western frontier scattered to Canada, Oklahoma and Wisconsin, but many Senecas settled at Buffalo Creek, now the city of Buffalo. Following the Treaty of Paris, new European settlers opened this frontier. The Indians were once more forced to move.

The Senecas, Keepers of the Western Door, no longer hunt and trade fur for their livelihood. Today, they are an economic force within New York State, recently acquiring some of their old Buffalo Creek grounds in the heart of downtown Buffalo.

Perhaps the words spoken in April 1792 by Good Peter, an Oneida leader, best sum up the aftermath for the Indians of New York State:

Emigrants Crossing the Plains. Using ox-drawn wagons, the pioneers traveled from the eastern states to make a new life in the wilderness of Western New York. *Courtesy of the Library of Congress Prints and Photographs Division.*

White Birds Cry

After this transaction, the voice of the birds from every quarter cried out:
"You have lost your country. You have lost your country.
You've lost your country! You have acted unwisely and done wrong."
And what increased the alarm was that the birds who made this cry were
white birds.

THE WAR OF 1812

O f the wars fought on American soil, the one that most involved Western New York was the War of 1812. During this conflict, troops were raised, forts won and lost, ships built and battles fought on four regional fronts: the Niagara frontier, the village of Buffalo and Lakes Erie and Ontario. As throughout its previous history, Western New York was a gateway through which the Americans could most directly attack Britain.

Britain was at war with Napoleon's Empire. Although American intentions on land and sea leaned toward neutrality, the Americans desired to finally be rid of British "colonial" presence. Since France had allied with the Americans during the Revolution, England feared that the Americans would come to France's aid in this conflict. Therefore, England set out to use its superior naval dominance to initiate a partial blockade of European ports to control American trade with France.

Seen as outwardly aggressive, this greatly displeased the Americans. Later in the war, the British would also blockade America's southern ports, making the eastern coastline one front in the war.

Even more offensive was the act of impressment. England, in need of additional troops, took British sailors by force from American merchant ships. American seamen were indiscriminately thrown in with the rest. The open sea became a second front in the conflict.

The final blow presented itself when Britain armed the Indians on the frontier, bringing the war uncomfortably close to the door of Western New York.

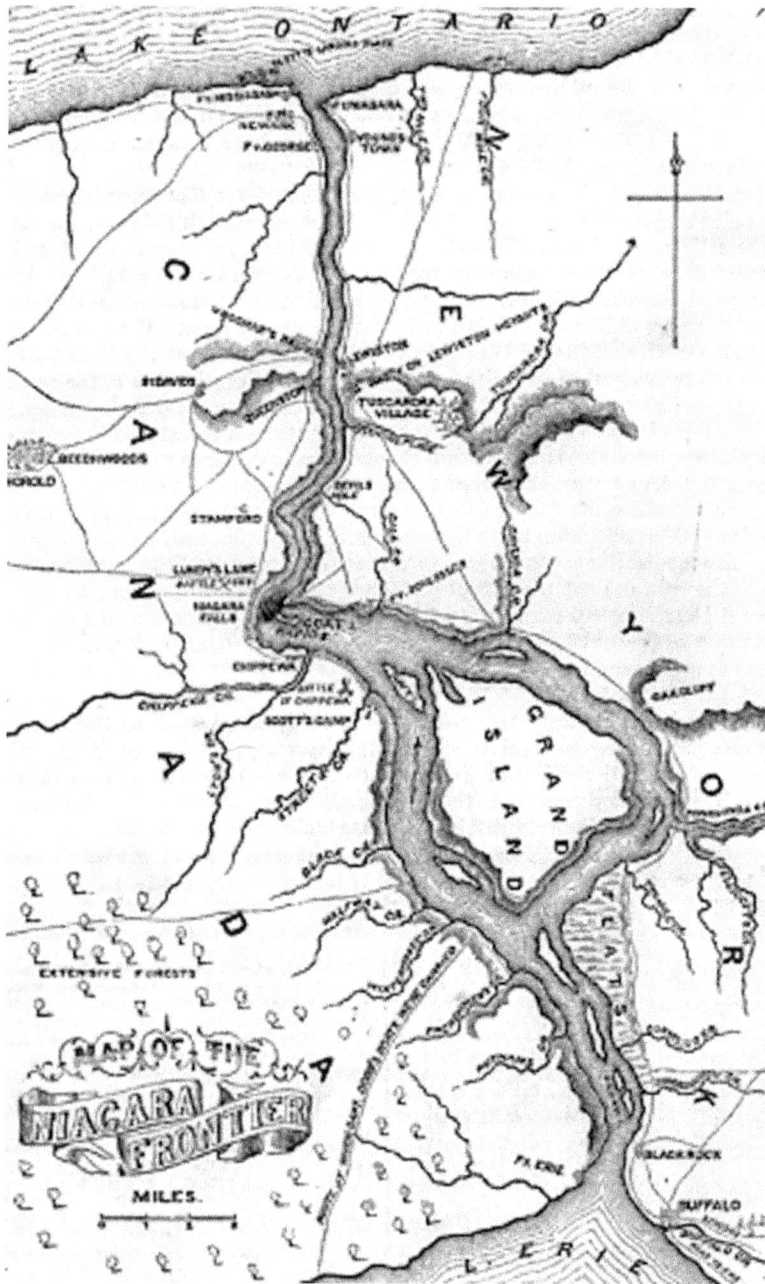

A War of 1812 map of the Niagara frontier.

The War of 1812

At the start of the War of 1812, the Americans lacked manpower and finances. New England had no real interest in becoming involved in a push to take Canada; in fact, it threatened secession. Britain took advantage of this division, forcing a blockade on southern ports instead of harassing New England. Actions to invade Canada were supported by President James Madison and a group of congressmen nicknamed the "War Hawks." Simultaneously, Britain had superior leadership and money to win such a conflict, but it was otherwise engaged with France. No troops were sent to defend its interests in Canada.

Because British Canada was sparsely populated and unprotected by sufficient British regulars, Madison and the "War Hawks" felt certain that it would be a simple task to take it. They hoped to end a border stalemate that in their eyes constantly threatened the United States and westward expansion. They were mistaken about how easily they could overrun Canada. Instead, the United States was dragged into what is considered by some to be our "Second War for Independence."

The Americans would gain an early upper hand for three reasons: 1) Britain was detained with Napoleon; 2) the Americans gained control of Lake Erie, cutting off support to the Indians; and 3) Major General Isaac Brock, a stalwart challenger during the first attack against Canada, was killed at Queenston Heights.

Not until Napoleon abdicated did Britain send an additional fifteen thousand troops to the continent, but by then the war was nearly over. Fatefully, perhaps, cessation of the war with France ended the very actions that first annoyed the Americans. Britain no longer needed blockades or extra sailors. The Indian confederation was broken, and peace negotiations soon followed. Neither the United States nor Britain would have a decisive win. Lands taken by both were returned to their former occupants with the Treaty of Ghent in 1814. A lasting peace followed. However, news of the treaty was not immediate since horse and rider were still delivering government messages and mail. A final battle ensued when American forces under Andrew Jackson successfully defended New Orleans from a British invasion.

Even though the Americans had not succeeded in taking Canada, their confidence was restored by victory at New Orleans. Both the Americans and Canadians would gain a sense of national pride following the war.

A NEW ENDEAVOR:
WAR SHIPS ON THE GREAT LAKES

Control of the Great Lakes meant victory in the war. At the onset, Britain had the advantage of many ships, while the United States had none.

Located north of Buffalo is a neighborhood called Black Rock, so called because of a nearby shelf of black limestone that rose four to five feet above the river. Once an independent settlement, Black Rock had a naval yard during the war. During the War of 1812, Black Rock saw three land battles and one naval action against the British.

Never before or again would there be such naval activity on Lakes Erie and Ontario as during this war. In fact, sailing ships at Black Rock were being fitted with guns for the first time in regional history. They included the schooners *Somers*, *Tigress* and *Ohio* and the sloop-rigged *Trippe*. However, they were unable to gain access to the lake with British-held Fort Erie just across the river.

The Americans' only warship, the brig *Adams*, was seized when General Hull surrendered at Detroit. It was renamed the *Detroit* in honor of that British victory. In October 1812, the Americans recaptured the ship and another called the *Caledonia* at Fort Erie. Ships changed hands throughout the war; some were destroyed, some ran aground and others were deliberately sunk.

CUTTING OUT THE *DETROIT* AND THE *CALEDONIA*

Built in 1764, Fort Erie was a supply base for Loyalists during the Revolutionary War. It stood at the headwaters of the Niagara River, where weather quickly decayed its structure. In 1803, planning began for a new Fort Erie just behind the old one. Construction was still underway when war was declared in 1812, but the fort was manned.

OCTOBER 9, 1812

The night was calm, with light winds. At one hour past midnight, two boats laden with one hundred men rowed with muffled oars out of Black Rock.

Commanded by Lieutenant Jesse Duncan Elliott, the boats glided toward Fort Erie. Poised on the opposite shore, the fort looked no more than a menacing shadow.

Two vessels, the British *Caledonia* and the captured *Detroit*, stood anchored under protection of the fort's guns. Elliott's daring mission was to cut them out, restoring the *Detroit* that was lost to General Brock and with it, America's pride. Both ships would add to the American fleet, and the *Caledonia*'s tidy cargo of furs would add to the coffers. Two hours later, after a brief battle, Elliott's crew boarded and captured the prizes.

Winds were too light for sails, so the vessels were drifted out into the current. The *Caledonia* sat light in the water, even with its cargo, and drifted easily to the American shore. The slower *Detroit* was immediately under fire of British artillery. Elliott dropped anchor, moved his guns to starboard and fired on the fort until his ammunition was depleted. Cutting anchor, the current urged the *Detroit* downriver, where it ran aground on Squaw Island, just off Buffalo's shore.

The *Caledonia* would bravely take part in the Battle of Lake Erie, but the *Detroit* was stripped of anything useful and set afire so that the British would not retake it. Some believe that the mighty Niagara demands two sacrifices each year; the brig *Detroit* paid the price.

Elliott not only took valuable cargo but also set free forty American prisoners aboard the ships while capturing seventy enemy sailors. In this bold cutting-out exercise, Elliott depleted Britain's fleet and the *Caledonia* became the American fleet's first ship. Furthermore, the nation was invigorated by the success.

Now, with more American support, the naval yard was moved from Black Rock to Presqu'isle (today's city of Erie, Pennsylvania, once a large Eriez Indian village). Gunboats were built under the watchful eye of mariner Daniel Dobbins, though his operations were poorly provisioned, with only one cannon and few men to protect the ships being built. Oliver Hazard Perry continued to be haunted by this after he took command of the fleet.

Lieutenant Jesse D. Elliott did not favor Perry's appointment over his own. He and Commodore Chauncey, a weak leader and Perry's immediate superior, would further Perry's frustrations. Yet Oliver Hazard Perry would prove daring.

Bloody Heights:
The Battle at Queenston

Lewiston, named for Governor Morgan Lewis, son of a signer of the Declaration of Independence, is located where the Niagara River exits the great gorge created by the falls over twelve thousand years ago. Located in Canada, Queenston directly opposes Lewiston. American Fort Niagara and British Fort George watched over each other.

Capturing Queenston was to be part of a three-pronged campaign to take Canada; the first campaign at Detroit failed, as did the second on the St. Lawrence River. Major General Stephen Van Rensselaer's attack on Queenston was now postponed. They should have crossed the Niagara on October 11, 1812, but Brigadier General Alexander Smyth, always ready to be a thorn in Van Rensselaer's side, managed once more to muddy the waters. That was no pun. It had been raining when he set out from Black Rock to join the general at Lewiston two days earlier. Western New York roads were not the best and mud bogged down his men and cannons. And why was Smyth in Buffalo anyway? thought Van Rensselaer. Hadn't he requested Smyth's attention at Lewiston days before? It was outrageous!

Smyth's audacity was remarkable. Even after Van Rensselaer delayed because Smyth's force was not present—and that scoundrel Lieutenant Sim deserted with the lead boat that stored all their oars—Smyth remained nowhere to be seen. Circumstances were ripe for an attack. Elliott's cutting-out mission of two British vessels at Fort Erie successfully inspired the troops. British General Brock, who had defeated the Americans at Detroit, was said to have left Niagara to repel a counterattack at Detroit. Yes, the time was ripe, but where was Smyth and his seventeen hundred men? When word arrived that they would not be ready until October 14, Van Rensselaer could wait no longer.

October 13, 1812

General Van Rensselaer's forces waited at the Lewiston ferry landing, damp and cold from a northeastern torrent that had blown in two days past. Van Rensselaer had only managed to hire fourteen boats, which had already carried two waves across. Now it was to be the militia's turn. Of the six thousand men he commanded in this operation, he valued his militia most.

Recent recruits, the regulars were hardly able to fasten their own shoes, and they gave him no respect. But these militiamen of the frontier were seasoned, and he needed them. Van Rensselaer returned from Queenston to urge them on.

Things were going poorly on the Canadian side of the river. The first wave of Van Rensselaer's men set out before daybreak, secrecy being their plan. However, a brief armistice that had allowed both the Americans and the British to make use of the river had foiled that plan. Brock's return to Detroit was a false report; he was, in fact, at his post in Niagara. General Brock watched for three days while Van Rensselaer gathered his forces and materials, including new oars. Van Rensselaer made reconnaissance to Queenston and by now knew the lay of the land, but Brock also knew that Van Rensselaer was coming. Brock had intelligence from Major Thomas Evans, who returned from requesting an exchange of prisoners from Elliott's raid held at Black Rock. He reported to General Brock at Fort George that he had been warily received and had noticed boats hidden among the bushes at Lewiston. He was certain an invasion was imminent. Redcoats and local Queenston militia were in place, with reinforcements already on their way by the time the invasion began.

In the dusky morning light, a vigilant sentry spotted American boats as they landed near Queenston Village and raised the alarm. Poised on the Heights, British musket brigades and artillery, loaded with grapeshot, cut to pieces the first wave of invasion. General Brock's arrival just at daybreak inspired the Canadians, further confounding Van Rensselaer's plans. As the sun rose, British artillery became more accurate, and three more American boats were forced to turn back. Rensselaer's movement stalled, and he was frustrated.

The second wave fared little better, for these boats were shot apart or drifted downstream to Hamilton's Cove, where they were immediately surrounded. American troops, who did set foot on shore, were either killed or taken prisoner. However, a fortunate turn of events had placed one command of the first wave secretly in an advantageous position. Because of a dispute over who should take command, the first wave had been split in two between Colonel Solomon Van Rensselaer and Lieutenant Colonel John Christie. Colonel Van Rensselaer was seriously wounded as his boat landed, so Captain John Wool took over the command. Some of Wool's troops, who were able to land, used a fisherman's path and cover of darkness to position themselves behind the British on the Heights. Coming from behind, they sandwiched the enemy between themselves and new American arrivals

War of 1812 soldiers. *Courtesy of the Library of Congress Prints and Photographs Division.*

on the shore. When in place, Wool attacked from the Heights, forcing the redcoats down into the village.

Seeing this, General Brock ordered his forces, under command of Captains Dennis and Williams, to push back, but the Americans pinned them down. Brock then ordered his aide-de-camp, Lieutenant Colonel John Macdonell, to "push on the York Volunteers." Brock bravely leapt from his horse and sponsored the counterattack. As he charged the hill, he was shot in the hand and then in the chest. Both he and Macdonell, along with Brock's horse Alfred, were killed. Dennis and Williams were seriously wounded, and additional American reinforcements aided the Americans in retaining the Heights. They un-spiked a British eighteen-pounder and used it against the village.

That brief victory on the Heights had taken place hours ago, at ten o'clock in the morning. It was now three past midday. Only about one thousand of Van Rensselaer's men had managed to cross. Waiting was unbearable for those still at Lewiston.

General Van Rensselaer had been there on the Heights, along with Lieutenant Colonel Christie and engineer Lieutenant Totten, to begin preparations for a fortification. Holding it was imperative, yet where was Van Rensselaer's beloved militia? Appointing Colonel Winfield Scott to take command of the three hundred or so American regulars on that high ground, General Van Rensselaer crossed back to Lewiston to inquire about the delay.

He quickly learned the answer to his question, and he did not like it one bit. With no boatmen to carry them to Canada, he found a disorderly rabble of grumbling, complaining, frightened militia and regulars ready to leave for home. They had been anxious to be engaged but waited for thirteen cold hours, listening to bombardment and musket fire that started before dawn. Added to that were cannons from Queenston exchanging fire with those at the small earthworks of Fort Gray and the chilling war cries of British-allied Indians. It was no wonder they had become less than enthusiastic. Word had gone around from a trained lawyer among them that their constitutional rights were being trampled; the militia could not be forced to fight on foreign soil. General Van Rensselaer was more than disappointed. Without them, he knew the day was lost. Word was sent to his commanders Wadsworth, and Scott on the Heights. They would be the ones to decide whether to continue fighting or make good a speedy withdrawal.

As Wadsworth and Scott received General Van Rensselaer's troubling message, British Major General Roger Sheaffe, who had marched his army in a three-mile detour to avoid American fire from atop the Heights, took position. Three hundred Mohawks, under natives John Norton and John Brant (Joseph Brant's son), retreated to the woods following an attack and

A view of Brock Memorial on Queenston Heights, as seen from Lewiston. *Courtesy of the author.*

joined Sheaffe. With the numbers on his side, he took his time organizing his men and munitions for a counterassault.

Wadsworth and Scott decided to withdraw and save what men they had left. Falling back, they attempted to throw up a barricade to cover their escape. Sheaffe's first attack an hour later was with militia and Indians against that barricade, which forced Scott's few remaining riflemen to flee. This was followed by an all-out attack. Van Rensselaer's mutineering militia, waiting at Lewiston, heard shots and war cries. The Americans on the Heights were forced to surrender. Wadsworth and Scott were taken prisoner, as were some sixty-seven additional officers. Winfield Scott would later be released and go on to fight other battles, including the assault on Fort George, the Battle at Lundy's Lane and, later, in the Mexican War.

While General Brock's death might have favored the Americans, in truth it created a heroic legend that rallied the Canadians in their efforts to avoid invasion. However, Brock was a crucial link to Tecumseh and the Indian Confederacy. His death aided the Americans in breaking that alliance. When Tecumseh died in 1813 at the Battle of the Thames, the confederacy crumbled.

The story of the Queenston Battle has all the twists and turns that make a good story—the American failure to take Queenston because of Brock's heroism, intense British fire, treachery or cowardice in the ranks and leadership. In addition to Smyth's absence and the militia's fears, accounts say that some American soldiers, understandably afraid of losing their scalps, came out of hiding in the woods on Queenston Heights when Scott raised a flag of truce. This stunned Scott, perhaps because he felt he could have won with their support.

One tragic account from a British officer tells of American soldiers on the Heights with their backs to the cliffs and no choice but to jump or surrender. Most surrendered, but as the account says, "They fell in great numbers." The swift, unforgiving river and jagged rocks waited below. In the midst of intense battle, Indians and British forces continued to fire on fleeing Americans, even after their surrender. The Americans lost over 300 men, with nearly 1,000 taken prisoner. The British fared much better, with fewer than 150 casualties.

In another twist of fate, General Brock had wanted to attack before Van Rensselaer could assemble what he needed but was hampered by the armistice and disagreement with his superior, Lieutenant General Sir George Provost. If he had taken offensive actions first, perhaps fewer lives would have been lost or the tables of invasion might have been turned. If the Americans embarking from Western New York had succeeded at Queenston, many believe that Canada would be an annex of the United States. Instead, a bridge connects the two countries at Canadian Queenston and American Lewiston.

Van Rensselaer resigned following this fateful battle, and Smyth took his place. Although Smyth made two additional attempts on Canada from his position at Black Rock, he too failed. His losses and treachery caused him to be despised by his men. Smyth "retired" to his home in Virginia. British general Isaac Brock was immortalized.

Before the war was finished, the British would indeed set foot on Western New York soil.

A Brief Occupation

Several battles and events took place following the American losses at Queenston that set into motion the eventual burning of Buffalo.

Winter arrived in Western New York following General Smyth's bungled attempts to invade Canada. A blanket of snow covered the ground, and although cannons kept a watchful eye, they slept until spring. April brought with it the usual promises, but for soldiers this was campaign season. It started in the region with a successful, though brief, two-day occupation of York (present-day Toronto). After burning many of the city's buildings, conquering troops returned to Fort Niagara to recuperate. They awaited marching orders that were to be for an assault on Fort George across the river.

The battle for Fort George on May 27, 1813, included using some of Isaac Chauncey's fleet on Lake Ontario under the command of Oliver Hazard Perry. Perry was commissioned to serve on Lake Erie, where he would later win fame. He had already begun building his fleet at Presqu'isle earlier that spring. Fort Niagara's cannons and supporting land batteries shared in the bombardment, using hotshot that set wooden structures within Fort George on fire. American forces won the fort. This victory is attributed to excellent planning and leadership on the part of junior officers Winfield Scott and Perry, resulting in the taking of not only one well-positioned fortification but also a second when the British deserted Fort Erie. This allowed Perry to bring ships blockaded at Black Rock into Lake Erie. Unfortunately, the Americans would leave themselves vulnerable as they continued their push into Canada. A defeat at Stoney Creek in June forced them to abandon Fort Erie and retreat to Fort George. They could make little use of these strategic victories. Another defeat at Beaver Dams, near Fort George, ended their advantage. Their greatest foil at Beaver Dams was not the trained British army but the courage of a woman, Laura Secord, British heroine of 1812.

Though the Americans could not have known it at the time, they nearly lost Fort Niagara, but British General Provost had been indecisive once more and the fort was not attacked. In July 1813, the British did raid Fort Schlosser, a small American outpost originally built in 1760 by the French near the upper portage of Niagara Falls. Nothing remains of this building today. By December, the British had regained control of Fort George. It remained in their hands until war's end.

There was one impressive battle left for the Americans before they gave up Fort George. Oliver Hazard Perry would be victorious in the largest naval battle on the Great Lakes.

BATTLE ON THE SALTLESS SEA

Daniel Dobbins was doing his best to defend the shipyard with only one cannon and few men. When Oliver Perry arrived at his new post, he could not believe his eyes. Nothing significant had taken place. The residents of the small village of Presqu'isle had mostly fled in fear of potential British raids. Where were the carpenters, ship joiners and other craftsmen promised him? Had he kissed his wife of two years farewell, asked for this transfer to the frontier, traveled through winter weather, all for this? Sometimes he felt cursed. The affair with the *Revenge* and his preliminary court-martial had been difficult enough. He had hoped that his time of inactivity and his new family would change his luck. This post was a chance to start again, but there was nothing here!

He could expect no real help from his superior, Commodore Chauncey, either. Dealing with Chauncey was useless; the man was a worrier not a fighter. Then there was Elliott from Black Rock. Yes, he had captured two ships, but he was forced to burn one, and because of his daring, Elliott believed that the command on Lake Erie should be his. Perry was fairly certain that the craftsmen Chauncey had sent him were not the best; Elliott had most likely netted the best of them. It was maddening. Well, he would do what he could.

The Battle of Lake Erie. Oliver Perry makes his way to take control of the *Niagara* from the treacherous hands of Jesse Elliott. *Courtesy of the Library of Congress Prints and Photographs Division.*

Perry traveled to Pittsburgh for help. With the aid of a friend, the naval agent in Pittsburgh, Perry's supplies, munitions and men began to arrive. The Pennsylvania militia was also sent to help protect his efforts. He gained some favor with Chauncey when the commodore asked him to take the fleet at Fort George. The five ships from Black Rock were now fitted with a few guns, adding to Perry's lake fleet. This addition had not been the easiest of tasks. It took over two hundred men and oxen to drag the ships against Niagara's currents and strong headwinds on the lake with British ships in pursuit. Only a fog that seemed to rise from nowhere helped him bring the vessels into Put-in-Bay. Perry's fleet now outgunned the British; still, Chauncey would not supply sailors.

Just as Perry received orders to attack the British with his new, not fully completed fleet, he also received news that a dear friend, Captain James Lawrence, had died in action. Oliver Perry named one of his two flagships the *Niagara* and the other the *Lawrence* in honor of his friend. The motto on Perry's personal battle flag read, "Don't Give Up the Ship," Lawrence's last words.

A few days later, after once again begging Chauncey to send sailors, Perry's cousin, Sailing Master Stephen Champlin, arrived with seventy men from Black Rock, consisting of militia and African Americans, among others who were not experienced seamen. At the end of July, he received sixty more men, mostly ill. His other men still struggled with "lake fever."

Despite all of these delays and obstacles by Chauncey, Elliott, the weather, illness and his own past demons, Oliver Perry led the attack on September 10, 1813. The victory on Lake Erie was so complete that every ship in Britain's Lake Erie fleet was captured. However, another tragedy befell Perry in the form of treachery.

Whether due to jealousy or cowardice, Elliott, who commanded the *Niagara*, kept his distance. Standing off, he did not enter the battle. Heroic to the core, Perry answered Elliott's treachery with bold action. Seeing the wounded and dying on the deck of the battered *Lawrence*, which had taken the full blast of British guns, he assigned control of the ship to what officers he had left and had his flag lowered. With four oarsmen in his gig, Perry ordered them to the *Niagara*. British ships, seeing him emerge from the smoke of battle, fired on the small vessel but missed. His newly found luck held, and soon he arrived alongside the *Niagara*, his banner in hand. After a strangely calm greeting from Captain Elliott, Perry relieved him of duty and sailed the *Niagara* into the fray and victory.

Thus ended Perry's proud ship the *Lawrence*, which was blown to bits in battle. While Jesse Elliott continued to command the Erie fleet until the end of the war, this controversy followed him beyond the grave.

From our past, Oliver Hazard Perry, "the Hero of Lake Erie," sends us his immortal words: "We have met the enemy and they are ours."

THE BURNING OF BUFFALO

After Oliver Perry's naval victory, the Americans sent their main force east for an assault against Montreal. This left only a few regulars and about one thousand militia under George McClure at Fort George. They were vulnerable to a larger British force stationed at Burlington and York, and at the same time, they angered nearby settlers by raiding their homesteads. McClure found it difficult to control his troops. To make matters worse, many had short enlistments that expired in early December. These men left for home, and with only five hundred or so remaining, McClure had little choice but to abandon Fort George and retire to Fort Niagara. Having been given permission to destroy the nearby village of Newark (now Niagara-on-the-Lake) if needed to defend Fort George, he gave residents only a few hours' notice and then ordered it torched to the last house. The inhabitants, mostly women and children, were forced into frigid December snows.

The British sought revenge upon hearing of this atrocity. American settlers were troubled, as British forces could be spotted gathering along the Canadian shore, preparing to strike. McClure had not only been cruel in his judgment but had also thrown down a gauntlet. He did not realize that British troops already marched toward the frontier when he made his decision. Even after pulling back across the river, he failed again by not considering adequate defenses. With several villages on the frontier, he could have raised a goodly number of additional men to serve, but he did not. McClure may as well have shined a beacon on Fort Niagara and the surrounding communities.

December 19, 1813, dawned cold, and the events that followed are frozen in time. The first objective of the British army was Fort Niagara. Its occupants were not prepared when the attack began, and the fort's commander, Captain Nathaniel Leonard, was three miles away at his home. The British made quick work of taking the fort. Sixty-five Americans fell, many to the bayonet. With the fortification now in British hands, more British crossed the river, bringing with them the Americans' greatest nightmare: several hundred Indians. Lewiston residents fled their homes just before hundreds of British soldiers and Indians flooded the village, demolishing, burning and plundering as they went. Residents who stayed behind were tomahawked; every farm or building along the river from Youngstown to Manchester (Niagara Falls) was torched. Fort Schlosser was also burned. The American riverbanks were lit with flames before the British tide was halted at Tonawanda Creek, where retreating American soldiers destroyed the bridge. Settlers breathed a sigh of relief, but the solace was not to last long. Ten days later, the British and their Indian allies set their sights on Black Rock and the village of Buffalo. A storm was coming, and little could be done to stay its fury.

It was Christmas season on the frontier, but it was without joy. Prayers were said and meals prepared, but the question on most minds was what to do and where to go when the British came. Fort Niagara was no longer a safe harbor for them. Many homes already lay empty, families having moved farther inland, seeking shelter with relatives or friends. Outlying settlers moved to nearby villages, where they could be better protected. Celebration was meager, if at all; hope for the new year was nonexistent.

British Major General Phineas Riall had only one plan. If it could be moved, take it; if not, destroy it, including all buildings that could shelter American troops. This also meant any ship wintering at Black Rock, where three of Oliver Perry's schooners were burned. Lieutenant General Sir Gordon Drummond, a less brutal man, ordered any man caught pillaging to be punished, but first they had to be seen. British soldiers captured the bridge crossing Conjocta Creek (Scajacquada Creek) at Black Rock.

Defenses went up at Buffalo as reinforcements came in from Genesee, Chautauqua and south of the village. Major General Amos Hall was to command these troops, and residents felt reassured. Hall had over two thousand men, including cavalry supplemented by one hundred or more militiamen from Buffalo under Lieutenant Colonel Chapin. December 28 was peaceful and quiet, and citizens of the village slept for the last time in the comfort of their homes.

THURSDAY, DECEMBER 30, 1813

Over one thousand of Riall's British troops silently crossed the river in the early morning hours. They landed at the foot of what is now Amherst Street, capturing a battery intended to protect the village, while a second division moved on Black Rock. Cannons at Black Rock cried the alarm and rent the morning silence as they tried to stem the rushing tide of destruction. General Amos Hall lost a few frightened deserters as he hurried to Black Rock to throw his remaining force of six hundred into the foray. They fought hardily but were forced to retreat back through Buffalo when Riall attacked their flank. Black Rock fell to the torch.

Most settlers in the village of Buffalo built their homes and businesses on Niagara Square's perimeters. Other homes were scattered along roads leading to outlying towns. Buffalo had two doctors, some lawyers, a few merchants and many taverns at Cold Spring on the Williamsville Road (now Main Street).

The sound of fleeing militia entering the village heralded dawn, and word spread that the British brought their Indians. Many residents gathered valuables and evacuated, passing warnings to other communities as they fled. Some inhabitants sought refuge at the Flint Hill farm of Judge Erastus Granger, a founding resident of Buffalo and an Indian agent. (His property served as a military encampment, and its location is marked with signage today.) Lieutenant Colonel Chapin and his militia stayed to fight.

A flood of British came by way of Guide Board Road (North Street) and Black Rock Road (Niagara and Mohawk Streets). Chapin tried to block them with a twelve-pounder at Main and Niagara, but his defensive only lasted a short time. The old cannon ceased its usefulness. Chapin, who tried desperately to arrange a surrender, was taken prisoner. Few residents or defending troops remained, except the dead and wounded.

THE MURDER OF MRS. JOSHUA LOVEJOY

Joshua Lovejoy homesteaded in Buffalo in 1807. He had been a tavern keeper at Avon but now had his own place on Washington Street with his wife, Sally, and their twelve-year-old son, Henry. They were proud of their hard work, their village and their country. When word came that the British had left Fort Niagara, Joshua mounted his horse, took his rifle and rode to the "Rock." If the British were burning as they advanced, he would see that his establishment, family, home and town were defended or give his life in the effort. Sally kissed her husband quickly and watched as he rode off in the dark. Henry stood by his mother's side, determined to protect her in his father's absence. It did not take her long to realize that her young son could not protect her but that she must protect him. Sally Lovejoy believed in all her heart that her gender would save her, but her son would raise his hand against the foe and they would strike him down. As soon as morning dawned, Sally sent Henry into the woods near their home and then sat waiting in her favorite chair near the fire.

Rage and revenge had been the battle cry of the British who crossed the Niagara. Their allies, the Indians, wanted only what they could take, including scalps that they could sell. They became Sally's unwelcome guests on that cold December morning.

Sally knew the enemy was near. She could hear them in every part of the village—British drums, rifle fire, whooping Indians. Her skin crawled with fear, but she would not give up her home. Perhaps they would just take the things she had not already hidden and leave, but she was mistaken. As the door burst open, the savages threw themselves at her. One took hold of the fine curtains she had sewn by hand. It had taken years of hard labor to make this house a home. Sally struck at him with a kitchen knife. A stroke—a single blow—from a tomahawk ended her dreams on the frontier. Her body was dragged from the house into the snow, where it lay for hours.

Sally Lovejoy was survived by her husband, Joshua. Following her murder, she was laid out in her home by kindly neighbors. According to one account, two days later the British and Indians burned her house with her body still inside. Upon his return, Joshua took his wife's ashes and buried them. He died in New York City in 1824. Their son, Henry, went on to become a prominent surveyor in Buffalo.

MRS. GAMALIEL ST. JOHN

Gamaliel St. John and his wife, Margaret, migrated from New England with a small army of children in 1807. They farmed in Williamsville until 1810, when they built a home and hotel in Buffalo. Margaret was a woman of extraordinary character, working very hard to keep her family safe and happy, even when burdened with heartbreak. She and Gamaliel lost a son in December 1812 to "camp fever." Then, tragically, in June 1813, Gamaliel and another son died in an accident on the river at Black Rock while ferrying supplies to American troops occupying Fort Erie. Only the very bravest of women could handle so much heartbreak in such a short time, and now she was threatened again.

Neighbors begged Widow St. John to flee before the British arrived. "They are taking everything, burning everything, killing everyone. You must leave." Refusing, she gathered her remaining eight children in the safest part of the house. Margaret somehow managed to get a message to British commanding officer General Riall, begging him to spare her home and property. For reasons we may never know, Riall left a guard over her. The home Gamaliel had made for Margaret stood fast during the onslaught and was the only residence not burned.

By three past midday, nearly all of the more than three hundred buildings in the village smoldered, leaving but a handful. Evacuees returned slowly throughout the night but were forced to flee again when the British returned on January 1. Only three buildings remained when they were finished: Mrs. St. John's house, a blacksmith shop and a jail. Leaving a garrison at Fort Niagara, the British returned to Canada with ninety prisoners. Over the days, weeks and months that followed the carnage, many Buffalo residents returned. They gathered over forty mangled frozen bodies, most having been stripped and scalped, and laid them out at the blacksmith shop to be claimed by family. In order to survive the winter months, many who stayed made do with what they had, building small shanties or roofing over their cellars. Some did not return until spring.

Spring brought more hardship for residents of the Niagara frontier. They not only had to prepare for planting but also had to rebuild their homes and lives. Although the landscape of the region had changed again, the spirits of these hardy people shone. Regular troops and residents staved off further attempts by the British to cross the river. By May 1814, a new town of Buffalo had taken form. Joseph Ellicott supplied $200 of his own money for "victim" relief. The Holland Land Company donated $2,000 more. In fact, relief came in from around the country.

Later, British General Provost issued a statement saying that he regretted having had to take such actions. He sarcastically admitted that it was less than friendly and against British character but added that the Americans had best behave themselves from now on. Yet the burning did not stop there. By war's end, many homes and public buildings in both countries would burn, including the White House in Washington, D.C.

The St. Johns' Williamsville farm had a spring that was the source of Mill Creek, a tributary of Tonawanda Creek. Their 1812 residence was located at what is now 460 Main Street in Buffalo. Margaret raised her children well following the war. All went on to have complete, rewarding lives.

The Coit House, oldest house in Buffalo, built in 1814. Pharmacist George Coit moved to Buffalo in 1811. He was one of many residents who had to rebuild their lives after the village was burned. *Courtesy of the author.*

War's End

The Americans captured Fort Erie in July 1814. Other battles would be fought in Canada at Chippawa and Lundy's Lane (Niagara Falls) during the summer months, but only one major battle took place on the Niagara frontier in the United States following the Buffalo atrocity, and that was at Conjocta (Scajaquada) Creek. This battle was the finest moment for the First Regiment of United States Riflemen, an elite unit that used guerilla tactics. At Conjocta, the regiment laid a trap using deception: they doubled back and ambushed the British before they could encircle Buffalo. Not much was left of Buffalo that was useful to the British, but the village had become an encampment for American forces. The victory at Conjocta was significant for the Americans.

Americans in occupation of Fort Erie withstood a siege of nearly one month before abandoning and destroying the fort in November 1814. At war's end in December 1814, Fort Erie was back in the hands of the British. The Americans returned to Fort Niagara in May of the following year. This was the last war on the Niagara frontier. The Erie Canal was about to open the region to expansion as never before seen. Later, the Industrial Revolution would once more change the region's face and its future.

HEART AND HARDY

Heroines of the War of 1812:
Laura Secord and Celea Sampson Cole

British Canadians have their heroine of 1812 in Laura Secord. Born in Massachusetts in 1775, her family moved to Canada in 1785 along with many loyal to the Crown. In 1797, she married Loyalist James Secord, who would later be seriously wounded near their home during the Battle of Queenston.

The Secords were forced to lodge American officers in their home following a second invasion of Canada in 1813. In June of that year, Laura overheard these officers as they plotted an attack on the British encamped at Beaver Dams. In secrecy, with her husband still convalescing, Laura made her way past enemy sentries and allied Indians and through wild woods and the dark of night to the headquarters of Lieutenant James Fitzgibbon to warn him of the American plan. Because of her courage, the Americans were defeated. Had they been successful in their attempt, they would have furthered their control of the Niagara Peninsula. Laura was eighty-five years old before she was given formal recognition for her daring deed.

Although lesser known, one year earlier, the Americans had such a courageous woman in their fold by the name of Celea Sampson Cole of Canadaway Creek.

Canadaway in Chautauqua County, approximately forty miles south of Buffalo, later became Fredonia or "Freedom." Canadaway's namesake, a derivation of the Indian word *Ga-na-da-wa-o*, meaning "among the hemlocks," was Canadaway Creek that feeds into Lake Erie. Even though the region is close to Canada, there really is no connection with the name.

Judge Zattu Cushing, a shipbuilder at Presqu'isle, sold a portion of his many acres to Seth Cole in 1805. This property was near the mouth of the creek. Seth, a Revolutionary War veteran, brought his wife, Celea, westward from Oneida County to become the first settlers in what is now Dunkirk. Exactly how many children they had when they arrived is uncertain, but some reports say that during their marriage they had ten children in all.

A wilderness at that time, the Coles had to clear the land to build their cabin and plant crops. In fact, Seth was instrumental in forming the region as he contracted with Joseph Ellicott, surveyor for the Holland Land Company, to make a road from the Pomfret line to Silver Creek.

It was not unusual in those wilderness days for settlers like Seth Cole to travel all the way to Manchester (Niagara Falls) to mill their grain at Porter's gristmill. What would take us an hour or so of highway driving would have taken a wagon at least two full days, perhaps more with layovers. Anything could happen in that span. During dangerous times, in war or storm, a settler would have preferred to remain at home to protect his property and family, but some chores could not wait. The Coles truly lived in the middle of no place and had to be hardy to survive.

Seth had died by the time war was declared by President James Madison in June 1812. Celea Cole was known by locals as Widow Cole. That July found her son Erastus stationed with the Chautauqua County militia at Lewiston. Celea was left alone with younger children to look after.

A frontierswoman's day began before sunrise. She lit a fire indoors for warmth during winter months and outdoors for cooking in the summer. There was always a pot of water heating—for washing, cooking and bathing. A barrel held rainwater, or else someone from the household made several trips per day to the creek, replenishing the water supply. Baking was done in the early hours to avoid summer heat, and laundry was a whole day affair. There was wood to chop, meals to serve and crops and livestock to tend, but if you were fortunate to have enough children, there were many helping hands to make the load lighter. The day's work ended with sunset. Even then, a frontier household might have a poor oil or rush light by which to do the sewing and other small chores not finished earlier. Summer in Western New York is almost as hot as winter is cold, mostly due to heavy humidity.

For Celea Cole, that July brought an unexpected adventure, when she would become an unlikely heroine in what some consider the first naval battle of the war.

Celea glanced out the cabin door to count the heads in Captain Tubbs's militia. Perhaps forty at best, she thought. It was comforting to have the militia here; she only wished her son was among them. How unfortunate that he had been sent to Lewiston. Still, these men were probably more than enough to guard any small boats carrying goods on the lake. Besides, the British had no purpose at Canadaway when American troops were amassing up north at Fort Niagara. Celea said a silent prayer for her son's safety and made up a second large trencher of food for the men. She was just carrying it through the door when shots rang out at the lakeshore. The militiamen snapped to, picked up rifles and ran toward the lake. Celea set the platter down and followed but kept her distance.

She smelled the gunpowder before clearing the trees where she saw a ship flying British colors anchored a quarter mile offshore. Panic hit her at the thought of Indians and scalping parties, but reason took hold when she didn't hear their usual war cries. She did, however, hear men shouting orders and the familiar crack of rifle and musket, broken suddenly by a resounding blast. Celea emerged from the tree line just in time to see the crewmen of an old salt boat that was run up on the sand reload the swivel-gun they had wedged in the crotch of a nearby tree. They shot at a British launch being rowed toward shore. Celea counted thirteen heads in the launch and noticed a flurry of activity on the anchored British ship. Her eyes met those of Captain Tubbs. She watched for a moment as Tubbs's men scrambled to the top of a low-rising sand bank, where they fired another volley at the redcoats. Captain Tubbs looked her way again.

Celea knew what she must do. Turning, she ran back toward her cabin and threw a saddle over her horse. She had told Erastus when he left that she would never really have much use for the creature and he should take it as a spare mount. "Where will I ride her? To the village? I could just as easily walk," she told him. It seemed like a waste then, but she was glad to have the horse now. Celea ordered her children to hide and rode toward the village with speed.

The alarm was up at Canadaway as soon as she arrived. Any militia still there hurried to the mouth of Canadaway Creek. Celea Cole, it is said, continued to feed and water the small army that fought off the British that day. Celea Cole, America's heroine of 1812, raised the alarm that brought aid to the salt boat crew. She may even have saved Canadaway from invasion.

Settler's First Blockhouse. A very common scene in the early wilderness of the Niagara frontier, settlers built near the waterways surrounded by heavy woodlands. *Courtesy of the Library of Congress Prints and Photographs Division.*

Accounts of the events that make up Celea's story are clouded. William Peacock of the Holland Land Company wrote, in July 1812, that the militia was placed at Canadaway Creek to guard against smuggling and trading with the enemy. Supposedly, someone was trading flour and potash, hoping to sneak it out to the British in the night. Yet another account places this incident in the year following the burning of Buffalo. Regardless, Celea Cole lived and died on the Western New York frontier. Her son Erastus survived the war and died in 1870.

THE ANGEL OF CHADWICK BAY

Solomon Chadwick gazed out over Lake Erie on a sunny, blue-sky morning. Gulls swooped and dove to catch the plentiful fish in the bay. He drew a deep breath, filling his lungs with the cool spring air, refreshing after a winter in his smoky cabin nearby. Solomon had brought his family to live near the harbor in 1810. Eventually, the spot would be named for him: Chadwick Bay at present-day Dunkirk.

Some stories say that Solomon was a friend to fishermen and sailors in the bay, but none says why he was known as such. The bay was not well known until eight years later, when it was considered for the western terminus of the Erie Canal. Yet people who lived along the shores of Lake Erie knew it to be one of the only suitable harbors for boats to land and therefore a danger when British ships prowled the region during the War of 1812. Some locals were known to harbor British for the purpose of smuggling, as reported in the story of Celea Cole at Canadaway Creek, another nearby inlet where small boats could land. Was Solomon harboring the British? It is doubtful. More likely, he knew the fury of Lake Erie and helped anyone in need. That beautiful morning on which he stood gazing could just as easily have brought one of the terrible storms on the Great Lakes. Any fishermen or sailor unlucky enough to be caught in a sudden Lake Erie storm would have been fortunate to land in that protected bay and have such an angel as Solomon Chadwick to help them.

In the end, the bay was not chosen for the canal, but in 1818 it became one of the ports for the *Walk-on-the-Water*, the first steamboat on Lake Erie. Perhaps Solomon and his son stood there when that steamboat pulled into port. They watched it unload its cargo of people and goods as the gulls dove and seemed to call out, "A new time has come!"

The region was progressing rapidly. Solomon eventually took his family to live in Perrysburg. In 1851, the New York and Erie Railroad made Dunkirk its end of the line, issuing in yet another new era.

STRANDED ON THE ICE

The day started out well enough as Zattu Cushing, his wife, Rachael, and their five children bundled up against the cold for the remainder of their journey west. Two hired men helped the Cushings harness the ox teams to the two sleds that would carry them and their household goods to Canadaway, their future home in Chautauqua County. Already, the family had traveled more than a fortnight from Oneida. The children were excited, but Rachael was apprehensive about the dangers they might yet meet. She recalled the day Zattu had hurried home from his last expedition to Lake Erie, announcing that he had purchased land in the most stunningly beautiful country he had ever seen. He reassured his wife that while there were Indians, they were friendly. And they were no strangers to the cold, having lived through lake-effect weather from Lake Ontario in Oneida.

"There is nothing to fret about," Zattu reassured her.

Rachael tucked her woolen shawl into the top of her skirt and Zattu's scarf about his neck.

"I know," she smiled.

It was February 1805 when the Cushings left Buffalo. That winter's morning they saw before them a sea of ice on the lake, upon which they planned to travel. Without sufficient roads, this was a common practice and was not troubling to them since they planned to be back on land by sunset. What the Cushings did not realize was that Lake Erie storms could come up suddenly, bringing with them an early darkness.

Throughout the day, they saw crevices in the ice and heard it cracking. As the wind picked up, a snowstorm brought an early nightfall. The hired men advised against continuing any farther without being able to see. The family was stranded.

The men pulled the oxen beside the sleds for shelter against the wind. The family covered themselves to stave off the bitter cold as wind temperatures fell to near below zero. Only an hour or two passed before Zattu realized the serious mistake they had made. His little family, while hardy like many pioneer families, would not make it through the night as they were.

Rachael dug through some of their goods and found the horn she used to call the children in for their supper. They took turns blowing on the little horn in hopes that someone in the night might hear them. It was just past midnight when their signal was heard. Two men traveling onshore heard the blast. With the aid of lanterns and careful strides, the two made their way to the Cushings and guided them and their belongings safely to shore at Eighteen-Mile Creek. They spent the rest of that night camped on land. At daybreak, what they saw took Rachael's breath away. As far as their eyes could see, the ice had broken into huge sheets that stood straight up at jagged opposing angles. They had come close to death that night, but now they safely completed their journey to settle in Canadaway.

Zattu Cushing did not get the land he had supposedly purchased. To his disappointment, Thomas McClintock was already living on it when the Cushings arrived. They lived for a time near the mouth of Canadaway Creek, but when McClintock moved in 1807, Zattu sold the creek property and finally took his Rachael to the spot he found so heavenly. They were home.

In 1808, Zattu was appointed associate judge for Niagara County, later becoming first judge of the Court of Common Pleas in Chautauqua County. He fought in the War of 1812, including a skirmish at the mouth of Canadaway Creek. Zattu remarried after Rachael died in 1816; they had eight children by that time. When he passed in 1839, his inheritance went to his second wife, Eunice, and her son, one of their four children together.

A true testimonial to a man's legacy is the fact that Judge Zattu Cushing fathered and grandfathered fine, upstanding children, some of whom would serve their country in the Civil War. His grandson William Cushing sank the ironclad *Albemarle* with a torpedo he designed himself. Alonzo Cushing died at Gettysburg defending the Union against Pickett's Charge. They say his dying words were: "I will give them one more shot, General Webb." Also serving in the same war with the United States Navy was another grandson, Milton Cushing. Yet another, Lieutenant Howard Cushing , was killed in an apache ambush in Arizona.

To think that the ice of Lake Erie might have ended that legacy before it began is a sobering thought.

Mail-Riding Mamma

Men and women carried the mail by horseback long before the mid-nineteenth-century Pony Express was developed, and the Niagara frontier was no exception. Because of the many dangers involved, this was usually a man's occupation, but occasionally a woman might need to take up her husband's work. It was not unusual for a woman of the frontier to sow, harvest, chop wood, hunt or anything else that was needed for survival if her man was laid up with sickness or injury. Sophia Williams, a Baptist sister from Canadaway, was one such woman.

Erastus Granger was named first postmaster of Buffalo Creek as early as 1804, with an office in Buffalo. Folks in the wilds south of Buffalo received their mail from points east through the Buffalo office, via Batavia; from points west through Erie, Pennsylvania; and from Canada via Niagara/Buffalo. Riders from outlying regions delivered and picked up parcels to carry elsewhere. Smaller communities had their drop-off points located in homes, taverns and other places of business. Post riders knew how to find settlers living in secluded areas, but sometimes mail went astray when a resident moved. For this reason, early postage was paid by the recipient, not the sender. In 1813, it cost twenty-five cents to receive a letter.

Sophia's husband, Richard Williams, rode the mail rounds from Buffalo to Erie on horseback. These excursions were rough, and one day in the year 1818, Richard returned home with the mail from Erie. He collapsed from illness and was no longer able to sit on his horse. His mailbag might have contained letters of deed on their way to the Holland Land Company office in Batavia, greetings from the west to loved ones in the east or marriage and death notices. Even then, the mail had to get through.

Sophia put her arm around Richard, hefted him to his bed and covered him with the quilt she had sewn to add color to their home. She opened the tin she kept atop the fireplace mantel that held a few tiny lozenges made of hemlock fruit covered in sugar to aid the taste. Sophia gave one to her husband, made him as comfortable as possible, stoked the fire and set out enough wood for him to bank it. Lifting the heavy mail pouch, she closed the door behind her. Outside, Sophia climbed on Richard's horse and rode toward Buffalo.

The spring thaw was on the countryside. Ice on the lake jammed some of the creeks as it began to break up on its way toward Niagara Falls and Lake Ontario. The hills of the southern tier poured their excess into feeder streams. The ground was still frozen in shady spots but soggy in others, prone to give way beneath a heavy horse. Sophia was lucky if she had a dirt road on which to travel, but even it would have been a muddy quagmire.

Flowing rapidly with drain off, Cattaraugus, Eighteen-Mile and Buffalo Creeks lay between her and her destination. Embankments that could be traveled in the dry summer were feet below the water that day. Sophia and the horse were soaked from head to toe as they splashed and swam their way across, but the mail arrived as dry as could be expected. Sophia held it overhead with one hand while she held the reins with the other, her knees firm about the horse's flanks.

An account of Sophia Williams was found in a Rootsweb ancestry record of the Baptist church in Fredonia. When she was still alive, she must have told her story to a friend, who in turn told it to the local record keeper. Sophia relayed that she had to make many such trips on Richard's behalf, doing so even when she had to carry her infant child along on that treacherous journey. As any strong frontierswoman might, Sophia held both the mail pouch and the child high enough to stay dry while crossing the creeks. Infused with good old American spirit, and born just three days after the signing of the Declaration of Independence, Sophia was the "mail-riding mamma" of Chautauqua County.

BILLY SHERMAN, CIVIL WAR VETERAN

Western New York played a role in the American Civil War, even though it was not fought on regional soil. Significant to Union security, with major waterways as well as a railroad center, there was a constant flow of soldiers, goods and supplies throughout the war. As with most parts of the country, the area sent its men to fight. Lives were lost and heroes were made.

Billy was the nickname often given to Union soldiers, but this Billy was a Confederate. His name was changed after he was captured at Chattanooga by Private Lorenzo Pratt, a bugler with the New York First Artillery Regiment, Battery M.

Battery M, part of the New York State regiment formed in Lockport, New York, in 1861, took part at Manassas, Bull Run, Antietum, the "Mud March," Chancellorsville and Gettysburg. It guarded supply lines on the Nashville and Chattanooga Railroad, and in late 1864, it followed General

William Tecumseh Sherman to the sea. The Federals were under constant fire for two months, and Battery M took part in every major engagement along the way. Its men were proud. They had lost men and seen bloodshed, but they had traveled all the way through Georgia and back to Washington with the general.

It was during the Battle of Chattanooga that Lorenzo Pratt met Billy. It is unknown how they fell in together or what Billy's former name might have been. Maybe Billy was a deserter, caught by Lorenzo when fleeing after his wagons or artillery were blown to bits by the Union army. Or it could be that Pratt, whose sole job it was to signal during battle, dropped what he was doing to take action as an infantryman when the enemy came so close that combat turned hand to hand. All that is known for certain is that Pratt changed his captive's name. He decided to call his new friend Billy Sherman in honor of his beloved general. Whether Billy liked it or not cannot be said, but the two of them stayed together for the remainder of the war.

The grave marker for Billy Sherman, captured Confederate horse. Billy Sherman's grave can be seen today on Wilson-Burt Road, just east of the village of Wilson. *Courtesy of the author.*

When Lorenzo Pratt was discharged from service, Billy went with him to live on his farm in Wilson, New York. They marched together in many community parades, and everyone loved them both. Billy helped Lorenzo on the farm, doing most of the heaviest work, until just three days before he died at age thirty. Truly, that's fairly young for a man, even a hardworking one, but Billy was no man. Billy Sherman was a captured Confederate horse, a dark bay, fifteen hands in height and loved by everyone who came to know him.

Billy Sherman was draped in an army blanket and his head was covered with the American flag. Someone read a poem about him as he was lowered into the ground on Lorenzo Pratt's farm, the place he had enjoyed in his older years. His grave was kept by aging members of the GAR (Grand Army of the Republic) for many years but was later taken over by the local historical society.

HORSEHEAD FIDDLES, HERMITS AND A FIDDLER'S GREEN

People who work hard tend to play hard, as did the pioneers of the frontier. Without modern conveniences of televisions, radios, computers, telephones and video games, the pioneers were obliged to make their own entertainments. They held barn raisings for new settlers, quilting and corn-husking bees and logging parties to clear the land, which were as much for fun as to lighten one man's load. These were social events, bringing distant neighbors together for a day of work, food, fun and sometimes competition. They began early in the day and lasted until sundown, when folks headed home. If enough people stayed for the night, the fiddlers rosined up their bows and everybody danced.

Country dancing was among the most popular pastimes, having traveled from England with the earliest colonists and migrated west with expansion. A fiddler and caller most often supplied music for these dances. Western New York callers were known for their singing-style calls. Communities on the frontier boasted of their fiddlers, always thanking them for their services because music lightened everyone's spirits.

The Holland Land Company was responsible for bringing settlers to Western New York, many of whom were surveyors and their families. Among them was twenty-one-year-old Amos Sottle, who arrived in an Indian canoe in 1796. Amos lived among the natives until his own cabin was ready. Settling into what must have been a lonely life, he became the first white settler in the current village of Hanover in Chautauqua County. In 1798, he began surveying that portion of the Holland Land Company's holdings. After his work was finished in 1800, Amos moved westward, following his trade to Ohio. He returned a few years later with ferryman William Sydney and a "black" woman, with whom he lived out his days. The story of Amos Sottle being the first white settler in Hanover is contested, as is whether his woman was African American or Native American, yet most agree that his fiddle was unique. It was made of a horse's skull.

Using materials available to create what was needed became a trademark among early settlers. They used local materials for their homes and placed local foods on their tables. Sometimes a man who wanted to play the fiddle had to use the materials available to him as well. For Amos, it was bone. There was a man named John Cuthbert, living at about the same time in England, who also made his fiddle out of a horse skull. While little is known of either man, apparently the idea of using a horse's skull to build a fiddle migrated from Europe. Moyles Hall, a museum in England, houses a collection of oddities, including a fiddle made of a skull. Originally thought to be a horse skull, it may actually be a cow's. Regardless, Western New York had such an instrument, and the community was grateful for Amos's playing.

MONGOLIAN LEGEND OF THE HORSEHEAD FIDDLE

The earliest origins of the horsehead fiddle seem to be Mongolian. Although not connected with Western New York, the legend explains the mystique that surrounds the idea of having a fiddle made in such a manner. Two versions of the story are found in Mongolia, where the musical tradition of playing the morin khuur, a cross between a fiddle and an upright base, exists even today. A horse's head is carved on the tuning head out of respect for the animal and because the sound is like a horse's neighing.

A shepherd named Kuku Namjil received a magical gift, a winged horse. Each night, Kuku mounted the animal and rode through the air to see his beloved. A jealous woman who wanted Kuku for herself hated the thought of him spending his nights with someone else. Patient, she waited in secrecy until the right moment. Before the horse came to Kuku one night, she hid among the clouds. When the horse flew past, she leapt from hiding and cut off the horse's wings. The poor beast was dashed upon the ground. Saddened by the loss, the shepherd shaped a fiddle of its bones and played beautiful songs in its honor. Anyone who listened heard the horse's voice as it neighed and felt its thundering hooves.

A second story says that a cruel lord killed the white horse of a young boy named Sukhe. That night, the horse entered the boy's dreams and told him how to make an instrument from its body. The first morin khuur was made with bones from the horse's neck, skin to cover the sound box and horsehair for the strings. When Sukhe played the morin, he was always with his beloved white horse.

Fiddling is associated with many Western New York villages. Named for Richard Stockton, a signer of the Declaration of Independence, the village of Stockton gave appreciation to John Ecker, its first village fiddler. The fact that records name him and his profession suggests the importance of music to the settlers.

Springville, another village in the southern part of the region, was named Fiddler's Green in 1815 by David Stickney, an original settler who operated the village's first hotel, the Tavern. He chose the village's name in honor of the fiddlers who played there. At one time, many fiddlers lived in the vicinity, such as David Leroy, a well-known fiddler, in 1812. His home near a green open space was a gathering place for fiddlers to learn and hold sessions. Fiddler's Green and its music were recognized as far away as New England.

Geneseo had a renowned fiddler as well. His name was Edward Peterson. Mr. Peterson was an African American Civil War veteran. He was best known for the typical Western New York "singing" call, which was very different from the usual "hollering" call in other parts of the country. In a 1926 interview, Ed recalled playing alone for dances all night until the wee hours of the morning. The calling tradition continued into the 1980s with "Accordion" Zeke, whom some considered a master caller.

Left-handed Charlie, the Hermit of Chautauqua Lake, always carried a fiddle, according to Lorraine Smith, who compiled an article on this eccentric. Charlie claimed to be quite the adventuring entertainer, saying he had been a "cowboy in the West, a sailor, a soldier, and a circus performer with the Dan Rice Circus." Lorraine writes that Charlie could imitate several instruments with his fiddle, including the piano and banjo. He played for many dances, always left-handed. Charlie lived sometimes on an island,

Interior scene, with a family gathered around a man playing a fiddle. *Courtesy of the Library of Congress Prints and Photographs Division.*

sometimes on a sailboat. He hunted and fished Indian style, cooked over a campfire and loved Chautauqua Lake. Charley Cowden, his given name, must have been a most colorful character, which only adds to the interesting history of Western New York fiddling. You can almost see him standing in the corner, stomping his foot as he played a lively tune! Charley passed away in 1908 and was buried in Pennsylvania.

Henry Ford, automobile entrepreneur, had a real interest in old-time fiddling, sponsoring many competitions. Charles Titus of Cattaraugus was a Henry Ford fiddler, weighing in at three hundred pounds. In 1879, the village of Canaseraga hosted the heavy men of the Erie Railroad and the "Fat Men's Ball," where the weight limit was no less than two hundred pounds. Other American cities hosted such events as well, showing the popularity of music, dance and any opportunity to socialize.

Early settlers on the Western New York frontier also enjoyed the hammered dulcimer. Many instruments from the nineteenth century still exist, attesting to their popularity. The Sackett dulcimer was made in the hamlet of Irving. But dancing, dance calling and fiddling are only the beginnings of Western

New York's entertainment legacy, which continues today. Once on the vaudeville circuit, Buffalo hosted huge names in the business, including many "black-face" minstrel shows. One of America's most beloved songs from these shows before the Civil War was "Buffalo Gals."

BUFFALO GALS

Originally written by John Hodges with the title "Lubly Fan" in 1844, the song was taken from city to city and the words were changed accordingly. When in Buffalo, it became "Buffalo Gals," and for some reason that title stuck. Although not written for Buffalo, it really speaks of the early Erie Canal–front atmosphere.

Buffalo Gals, won't you come out tonight,
Come out tonight, come out tonight.
Buffalo Gals, won't you come out tonight
And dance by the light of the moon.

As I was walking down the street,
Down the street, down the street,
A pretty little gal I chanced to meet,
Oh, she was fair to see.

I stopped her and we had a talk,
Had a talk, had a talk,
Her feet took up the whole sidewalk
And left no room for me.

I asked her if she'd have a dance,
Have a dance, have a dance,
I thought that I might have a chance
To shake a foot with her.

KITTY O'NEIL:
WORLD CHAMPION JIG AND CLOG DANCER

A minstrel and variety show town, Buffalo hosted burlesque performers as well. A canal boatman once told the story of having seen a beautiful naked dancer at the Canal Street Theatre on July 4, 1881. He said her name was Kitty O'Neil, but was she *the* Catherine "Kitty" O'Neil, singer and performer?

Catherine, commonly called Kitty, was so well loved that a fiddle tune was written in her honor. A seven-part fiddle showcase tune, "Kitty O'Neil's Champion Jig," became popular not only in America but in Ireland as well. More commonly known as "Kitty O'Shea" because it was misnamed on a Donengal recording by champion fiddler Tommy Peoples in the 1970s, the piece takes its more modern name from a nineteenth-century Irish mistress.

First appearing at the Canterbury Music Hall on Broadway in 1862, Kitty found herself embroiled in "the Concert Saloon Bill," a law enacted by those who disliked the "immorality" of the burlesque performances in the Broadway music halls. Many of the performers were labeled as "low-lives." Although the Canterbury in New York was considered a grand place in comparison to many others, the law put the theatre out of business, leading to the birth of many "legitimate" variety theatres. The difference between these theatres and their early cousins was their source of income from box-office sales rather than liquor. This attracted more female customers. For Kitty, it meant mastering a variety of skills—from singing and dancing to acting—in order to keep up with the change. A protégée of Broadway great Tony Pastor, she may be best known for the song "No Irish Need Apply."

Kitty's New York performances waned, eventually ending in 1888 at age thirty-seven, when she was considered too old to continue. After a failed marriage to Harry Kernell, Kitty moved to Buffalo and later married Alfred Pettie, a local restaurant and saloon owner in 1892. Kitty O'Neil, Broadway star and "the World Champion Jig and Clog Dancer," died at Buffalo General Hospital following complications from kidney stone surgery.

Over the years, Kitty O'Neil inspired many dancers who took her name and imitated her work. One wonders if the canal boatman's Kitty O'Neil, who danced naked on a twelve-inch pedestal for one hour, was *the* Kitty

O'Neil or an imitation. Or was the dancer at the Canal Theatre just a canal boatman's fantasy? We may never know, but burlesque was alive on the waterfront, with all of its wild women and burly canallers. Fine theatre was also alive for the "uptowners," and Buffalo continued to be on the main performance circuit.

VAUDEVILLE, THEATRE AND THE SILENT PICTURE

Vaudeville grew out of the Industrial Revolution following the Civil War and the need for family entertainment, perhaps an alternative to the more sordid burlesque entertainments available at the time. At vaudeville's high point, there were over four thousand theatres nationwide, with many in Western

The Riviera Theatre is still in use today, with concerts on its famous Wurlitzer organ. *Courtesy of the author.*

I'm So Glad You've Found Me: Oh, Take Me Away! Courtesy of the Library of Congress Prints and Photographs Division.

New York. Among them was the Grand Theatre in Buffalo, which was on the Orpheum Circuit controlled by Benjamin Franklin Keith and Edward F. Albee, both formerly employed with circuses. Opening many luxurious establishments, they censored speech, costume and promiscuous behaviors. Other vaudeville theatres in the region were the Fredonia Opera House, Lancaster Opera House and Lafayette Square Playhouse (later a movie house, torn down in the 1970s).

Vaudeville's popularity slowly declined with the advent of the silent movie. Western New York boasted of Vitascope Hall, located in Buffalo's Ellicott Square Building, the world's first movie theatre built specifically for that purpose. Silent films ushered in a whole new form of architecture in the region as beautifully decorated theatres were built, including Shea's Buffalo, the Savoy, the Sattler (with the same name as Sattler's Department Store), the Abbott, the Frontier, the Mirror (a nickelodeon), the Circle, the

Paramount, Palace Theatre (Lockport) and the Majestic Theatre, where the first full-length Technicolor feature, *The Gulf Between*, premiered in 1918. In addition, there was the Riviera, "showplace of Tonawanda." Music was an integral part of the silent picture, giving rise to the use of the organ. Nothing says organ better than Wurlitzer. Located in Tonawanda, the Wurlitzer Company later produced the rock 'n' roll era's most beloved jukeboxes, true gems in the crown of the Tonawandas.

The region's claim to entertainment fame does not stop with its theatres. Western New York has produced some of the nation's best-known actors and journalists, including James Whitmore (graduate of Amherst High School); Tim Russert; Reed Hadley (graduate of Bennett High School, Buffalo), who played Zorro; and, of course, the queen of comedy, Lucille Ball, from Jamestown. Not to mention myriad famous songwriters and musical performers such as Jack Yellen, who wrote "Happy Days Are Here Again," "Ain't She Sweet" and "My Yiddishe Momme," a song for one of America's most popular entertainers, Sophie Tucker. He also worked, at one time, with Harold Arlen, one of the world's most famous Buffalo songwriters, noted for the immortal "Over the Rainbow." Is it possible that Arlen was inspired by the rainbows that constantly form over Niagara Falls? It may be that the waterway so important to forming the Western New York landscape also touched many beyond its borders through this song.

THE BUFFALONIANS AND THE CRYSTAL BEACH BOAT

Harold Arlen was born Hyman Arluck on the East Side of Buffalo in 1905. Buffalo was in its boom years. The Erie Canal had done its job carrying goods between the Hudson and the Great Lakes, creating commerce and new settlements. Hydroelectric power harnessed the wild Niagara. Buffalo streets were lit with electric streetlights. In 1901, the Pan American Exposition left its mark, not only with the tragic assassination of President William McKinley but also with the beautiful landscaping of Delaware Park and incredible new architecture. Frank Lloyd Wright would soon build the notable Larkin Building and the Darwin Martin House. The city's population had topped 300,000, with immigrants from Germany, Italy, Ireland and Poland working in its steel and grain mills. The region was buzzing like a beehive, only slowing when something remarkable, perhaps even melodic, captured its imagination. Harold was born at the right time to be who he would become.

As a child, Harold enjoyed singing. His father was a cantor for the Pine Street Synagogue, and his mother hoped her son might someday become a music teacher. When still a young boy, Harold was more musically inclined than his own piano teacher. His parents found him an even more prominent tutor, who could show him how to conduct and compose. Not so interested in the teaching exercises he was given, Harold was fascinated with contemporary music of the period. He loved the sound of ragtime rhythm and experimental harmony. As a young boy growing up during the early days of silent movies, Harold took up playing for neighborhood movie houses and local vaudevillians. At age fifteen, he worked in some of the seedier playhouses in the city with his first band, the Snappy Trio. Harold dropped out of school when he was just sixteen to further his interest in music. His parents insisted that he continue his education, so Harold attended a vocational school to placate them. In just a short time, the trio grew to a five-piece band, the Southbound Shufflers. In 1923, Harold had his first experience playing on the Crystal Beach excursion boat, the *Canadiana*. Later, he joined the Yankee Six, which eventually became the Buffalonians, one of the best-loved bands in the region.

While playing at Geyer's, a ballroom in downtown Buffalo, Harold befriended a dancer named Ray Bolger. About 1925, the band began a nationwide tour that took it to all the hottest spots, including New York City, where Harold once more ran into his friend Bolger. Harold still loved singing, preferring it to composing, but it was his talent to arrange music that got him the most recognition. Harold left the Buffalonians. After a brief stint with another band, he became a solo vaudeville act. His career as a singer and songwriter, as was the case for many other great performers, was not an easy or a straight road, yet Harold's momentum brought him to Hollywood and Broadway, where he wrote some of the best-loved songs in musical history: "Come Rain or Come Shine," "Paper Moon," "Stormy Weather," "Get Happy," "World on a String," "Let's Fall in Love," "That Old Black Magic" and "Over the Rainbow."

One of Western New York's greatest treasures, Harold Arlen died in 1986 but did not come home to rest. He was buried at Hartsdale, near New York City.

COLORED MUSICIANS CLUB

Formed in 1918, one of Buffalo's longest-operating music organizations is the Colored Musicians Club. Born out of the desire for a musician's union that would include "colored" musicians, a new union was formed in 1917, leading to the opening of the club facilities. Currently located on Broadway in Buffalo, the club received its charter, incorporating in 1935. The club continues to be a place for all musicians, regardless of color, to jam and learn from one another. Many greats are known to have dropped in on their way through town, including Ella Fitzgerald, Count Basie, Dizzy Gillespie, Art Blakey, Duke Ellington and the immortal "Lady Day," Billie Holiday. You can almost feel it: a hot summer evening on the city street, the Buffalo humidity so thick you can cut it with a knife and the cool tones of Ms. Holiday drifting through the doorway into the night air: "Summertime, and the living is easy" and "Ain't nobody's business if I do." Ahh, satisfaction.

Western New Yorkers are grateful to all of the performers and musicians who have made good times better and hard times easier, people such as "Ramblin' Lou," a country musician and owner of WXRL radio station, and Earl Northrup, who operates Earl's restaurant in Chaffee, which has a history of musical performances by some of country music's greats. We thank those who have kept the region's musical legacy alive throughout the years, but it is not all about old-time country music, vaudeville and jazz. Western New York also prides itself on many twentieth-century musicians, including rock 'n' roller Big Wheelie; renowned harmonica player Shakin' Smith; the "King of Funk" Rick James; songwriter and founder of Righteous Babe Records Ani DiFranco; Jamestown's 10,000 Maniacs; and the Goo Goo Dolls, whose philanthropy has helped many underprivileged local youth.

What began with the story of a waterway and a region picking itself up from the ashes of war has become a place of inspiration for the world, an example set not only by courage and music but also by ingenuity.

HIYO SILVER—AWAY!

Seeds for the invention of the telegraph began in the late 1800s. The telegraph had been an important aid during the Civil War and expansion westward. As a result of telegraphy, the world saw a plethora of new technologies unfolding: the telephone and phonograph, leading eventually to the radio.

Heart and Hardy

American entertainment included a wealth of storytelling via the airwaves, with New York State's first stations starting in the early 1920s; Buffalo's started on March 25, 1922. The city had not only a significant local and regional effect on in-home entertainment but a national one as well, thanks to Francis Hamilton Striker.

Senior adults, once children of the early days of radio, still recall the excitement that came with their favorite programs. Families gathered in the parlor, some in rockers, on davenports or in easy chairs pulled up close, with children on the floor in front of the family console. All ears focused and eyes stared eagerly at the set, almost as if there would be a picture to see, but the pictures were all in their imaginations. Locally, one might have heard, "This is Clint Buehlman from the eighteenth floor of the Statler Building. It's a bright sunny morning in Western New York."

The box in the parlor brought national news from "the War," music, comedy, adventure and variety, without needing to leave the comfort of home. Families enjoyed the likes of Jack Benny; Bing Crosby; Bob Hope; Abbott and Costello; *Amos 'n' Andy*; *Our Miss Brooks*; *Jack Armstrong, the All-American Boy*; *Gang Busters*; and *The Shadow*. Children eagerly awaited to hear the weekly installment of "Hiyo Silver—Away!," *The Lone Ranger*.

Children across the country flocked to their radio sets to listen, donning their very own cowboy and Indian wear, featuring their

A boy ready to listen to *The Lone Ranger. Courtesy of Thomas Heim.*

trusty six-shooters and masks. Yes, the Lone Ranger, that legendary western hero who fought the bad guys with his sidekick Tonto, was a Western New York original, created in Buffalo by writer extraordinaire Fran Striker.

Striker began working on *The Lone Ranger* in 1932, a time when the world needed such heroes. The first episode aired on January 30, 1933, followed by almost three thousand more stories in the series. *The Lone Ranger* also made the transition into television, thrilling audiences of the Baby Boomer generation. The two companions, the Lone Ranger and Tonto, lived a very long life, until the time they slowly disappeared into the sunset like all other heroes at the end of a good day's work.

Fran Striker, born in Buffalo, a graduate of Lafayette High School and the University of Buffalo, also created *The Green Hornet* and contributed to *The Challenge of the Yukon* (the basis for the television series *Sergeant Preston of the Yukon*). Fran Striker, the man who created legends, was buried at Arcade Rural Cemetery in Arcade, New York, yet his legend continues.

> *The Lone Ranger is camped outside of town in a grove of cottonwood trees. Tonto, his trusted companion, scouts the area and reports back to Kemo Sabe.*

Such a lasting impression was made on listeners that even today the phrase "Who was that masked man?" can be heard. Real fans then think to themselves, He didn't say, but he left this silver bullet.

SHE DEVIL

The mighty Niagara has a strange power over people. Many say that it hungers for a yearly sacrifice, or perhaps gazing too long into the falls can boggle the mind and spellbind the viewer.

It was not until peacetime following the War of 1812 that the first attempts to survive the falls were recorded. Most of these early daredevils were interested in the challenge and the thrill, as it was always necessary to be the "first" at something in order for anyone to care. They wanted fame. The barrel riders almost always had slogans and advertising on their barrels. After all, someone had to sponsor them, or perhaps they had a statement to make. Whatever their reasons for taking such risks, some survived and some did not.

Heart and Hardy

As early as 1827, the dilapidated schooner *Michigan*, painted to look like a pirate ship with dummies on the deck, was sent over the falls, fully loaded with live animals. It was a tourism stunt perpetrated by one of Niagara Falls' first hotels. Needless to say, it did not go well for the animals, and the event was a complete fiasco. The only survivor was a goose.

Sam Patch also attempted the falls. He survived a dive over the falls, but when he tried the same thing in Rochester in the Genesee River, he drowned. A present-day Erie Canal excursion boat is named after him.

Many more "He Devils" tempted fate, but in 1901, it was a "She Devil" who would be the first to survive the trip in a barrel. Annie Edson Taylor was a schoolteacher. Like so many industrious people of the region, Annie filled in at various jobs to supplement her teaching income but suffered personal disasters that left her penniless. Why would an educated person even contemplate the life of a daredevil? Annie may have been desperate, or perhaps she always harbored a secret desire to be in the limelight. She may have seen success at going over the falls as a means of cementing a regular income. It would mean a sponsor and some amount of money. Annie even had an agent.

The barrel used was made of oak reinforced with iron and padded with a mattress. (Can you imagine today's mattress companies using this as a gimmick to sell a good night's sleep?) Everything that could be done to secure her barrel was tried. A few days before Annie used it, a domestic cat was sent over as a test. The cat made it safely. Now, it was Annie's turn.

Once Annie was inside the barrel, the lid was sealed, the barrel was pressurized using a bicycle pump and the hole was plugged. She must have been able to feel the bobbing motion of the barrel as it neared the falls, and she must have heard the thundering waters as her fate drew closer. One can only imagine the kind of stress that might cause. So much could go wrong! The barrel could crash on rocks, dashing Annie to bits. The barrel might be forced underwater and not surface until she ran out of air. The lid might not be as secure as they thought, and Annie could spill out of it even as the barrel floated to safety.

Huge crowds had gathered at the base of the falls to watch this daring deed. Nobody had tried such a thing before, and people were certainly amazed that a woman would be the first. They held their breaths.

In less than twenty minutes, a barrel was seen at the crest of the falls. People cheered and pointed; women bit their knuckles, shutting their eyes, afraid to look but still wanting to know. Was she alive? Yes! It took a while for the barrel to be fetched and opened, but Annie Edson Taylor stepped out

Daredevil Bobby Leach. Hundreds challenged the falls, and each outdid the other in method and equipment. Bobby's barrel was more elaborate than the plain wooden one used by Annie Taylor. *Courtesy of the Library of Congress Prints and Photographs Division.*

with nothing more than a scratch. She later said she that would never advise anyone else to do such a thing.

Annie made enough money as a speaker to subsist for a while, but she spent most of her remaining years posing for tourists at her souvenir stand. Annie died at age eighty-three without the fortune she had hoped for, but perhaps she had what she really wanted: a legacy as the first She Devil to go over Niagara Falls in a barrel and live to tell about it. Amazingly, when Annie took the plunge, she was sixty-three years old.

Annie would not be the last to try conquering the mighty Niagara. The last barrel ride over the falls was in 2003, and each year, in one way or another, the falls or the rapids below kill several people. You might say that the river has been calling since the day it was born and will probably do so until the end of time.

FLIGHTS TO FREEDOM

After the War of 1812, the next big event that would change the face of Western New York was the decision to make Buffalo the western terminus of the Erie Canal. Boats on the canal carried produce, lumber and other goods east, while bringing immigrants west by the thousands. From Buffalo, they could travel on ships into America's heartland. They came from Poland, Germany, Italy and Ireland, as well as other countries, to make a new life in a new land. In fact, many Irishmen worked as diggers building the canal, which began at Rome, New York, in 1817. It officially opened on October 26, 1825. Without all of these new people, the country could not have grown. They brought not only themselves and their families but also their skills and cultures. America and Western New York did indeed become "melting pots."

The intrepid fortitude of Western New York people helped them rebuild the villages that had been burned or looted during the War of 1812. With the infusion of these immigrants, the region hummed with activity. Canalboats from the east and sailing vessels from the west created a natural business environment for growth. People became wealthy from their endeavors, but the waterways brought a darker aspect. Buffalo's canal district became a place that respectable people shunned. The foul-talking boatmen, with all their filth, lurked there with the poor, the women of the streets, robbers and others, but it was indeed a place of bustling commerce.

Later, the American Civil War brought its soldiers into the mix, with Fort Porter (now a marine reserves base) and Fort Niagara upgraded with new garrisons. These soldiers were needed to protect the canal, rivers, lakes and railways from raids by Southern Rebels. Because England sympathized with the breakaway states, the troops also kept a wary eye on Canada.

People of color came, too. Prior to the war becoming official, when the sabers were still being rattled, slaves who had either escaped or been freed moved northward, many settling in Western New York. Among the best known was Joseph Hodge, also known as "Black Joe." He was the first black settler at Buffalo Creek in 1792. Another was William Douglas, from Tennessee, who arrived in the early to mid-1800s. He became the proprietor of the nefarious establishment Dug's Dive in the canal district.

Settling in Northern communities was common; many blacks started families and businesses, farmed and assimilated. All of that changed with the Fugitive Slave Laws of 1850, signed into law by Buffalonian, President Millard Fillmore. While laws allowing for the return of fugitive slaves across state lines had been in place as early as 1793, the civil unrest of the mid-1800s led to more aggressive cross-border bounty hunting. The escaped slaves were no longer safe in Northern states. All a slave hunter had to do was produce a reasonable amount of evidence and he had every right to use whatever force necessary to recapture those slaves and return them to their owners for "justice." Truth be told, free blacks were not secure either. Many were wrongly accused of having escaped or were outright kidnapped. Because of this, many blacks were determined to move still farther north into Canada.

Abolitionists who wished to end slavery helped many escape in such a way. This was the UGRR, the Underground Railroad. Many runaways followed it by way of a natural compass—the big dipper, or the "drinking gourd."

When the sun come back and the first quail calls,
Follow the Drinkin' Gourd
For the old man's waitin' for to carry you to freedom
If you follow the Drinkin' Gourd.

Blacks, whose very lives depended on successfully reaching the mighty Niagara, were assisted northward through Chautauqua County to Buffalo and on to Canada. From the east, they traveled along the Erie Canal to Lockport, New York. The hardiness of these escaped slaves cannot be denied. As slaves, they were disenfranchised but for the most part knew where their

The effects of the Fugitive Slave Law. Slaves were brutally returned to their masters, along with free blacks who were captured indiscriminately. *Courtesy of the Library of Congress Prints and Photographs Division.*

next meal would come from and where they would rest their heads on any given night. As escapees, they did not even know what waited around the next bend. Armed only with secret codes and stories that told them the way, these brave souls embarked on an unknown journey with the greatest of purpose in their hearts, something this country was founded on: the right to be free. They were the "freight" on this secret railroad, and they traveled the "lines" until they reached a "station." The people who helped them, "the conductors," also risked their lives and reputations. Literally hundreds of local citizens, whites and blacks both, did so, knowing that they could lose everything. Because of this, many names and details of their stories remain unknown.

> *The river bed makes a mighty fine road,*
> *Dead trees to show you the way*
> *And it's left foot, peg foot, traveling on*
> *Follow the drinking gourd*

Western New York was truly a hotbed of subversive activity, with estimates of at least thirty thousand slaves smuggled through the region to Canada over the years. They traveled to Buffalo, where they crossed the river either by boat or the one-time suspension bridge at Black Rock. Braving the currents, some swam. Well-known abolitionists spoke in Buffalo, including the son of a slave, Frederick Douglass, who visited on many occasions.

One escaped slave who became a prominent Buffalo resident, settling here in 1836, was a man known in the South simply as William. He was to become a very verbal abolitionist conductor on the Underground Railroad, taking a new name after a Quaker, Wells Brown, who helped him in his escape. William Wells Brown is attributed as the first African American novelist. Another name to recall in the story of freedom is Sojourner Truth, who was also helped by the Quakers and became an outspoken voice. Sojourner was welcome in many Western New York homes.

Dug's Dive, with all its glorious dankness and shady waterfront characters, may also have been a safe harbor for slaves who "followed the drinking gourd." It was well off the beaten path and was not frequented by whites, other than the usual canal rabble. Located at that time in a basement in the Union Block, or "Negro" district, the saloon was accessible only by entering from the canal towpath. Demolished at the end of the nineteenth century, along with the Union Block, Dug's Dive would have been the perfect place for runaways once they arrived in Buffalo. Many had to wait for appropriate times and cover of night for that last leg of the journey across the river to freedom. Farms, homes and even businesses throughout the region used secret cellars, attics, barn floors, wit and trickery to hide fugitive slaves.

> *I thought I heard the angels say*
> *Follow the drinking gourd*
> *The stars in the heavens gonna show you the way*
> *Follow the drinking gourd*

The Religious Society of Friends, or Quakers, also known as the Friends, were among the many who put the heart in the story of Western New York by aiding runaway slaves. Formed in England during the seventeenth century, the Quakers continue to live a simple life, according to the requirements of their individual communities. They extended their hands in friendship to all in need. When slavery became a serious issue, the Quaker population proclaimed their allegiance to the abolition movement. It was forbidden to act in any way that would acknowledge the right of slavery. Many boycotted the use of cotton cloth and white sugar, along with other goods that might be produced with unpaid labor. Further, when the Fugitive Law made it illegal to harbor slaves, the Friends obstinately denied the law's significance. In other words, they ignored it.

The Quakers were not the only Chautauqua County residents to assist slaves in their flight to freedom. Antislavery leaders such as Benjamin Wade and Joshua Giddings had ties to the county. Jamestown, New York, which is located at the eastern tip of Chautauqua Lake, actually had a large settlement of free blacks that locals called "Africa." A resident of this settlement, whose home is marked by signage for its use as a station, was Catherine Harris.

Born a free black in Meadsville, Pennsylvania, Catherine moved to Jamestown with her young daughter in the mid-1800s. They were the first people of color to live there. By 1849, there were almost one hundred blacks living in "Africa." Some were runaways; some were spies for the slave hunters. Numerous runaways were recaptured, and even free blacks living in the settlement were taken. Catherine did what she could to hide the fugitives in her home. For her courage and kindness, and because she was a prominent citizen of Jamestown, her grave site in Lakeview Cemetery is marked by a monument.

DRAFT RIOTS

The history of the 1863 draft riots in New York City is familiar. From July 13 to July 16, several militia and volunteer troops took to the streets under President Lincoln's orders to control the chaos. What had begun as an angry protest became a lawless free-for-all, with countless blacks murdered and a black orphanage destroyed. On July 6, exactly one week prior to these horrible events, Buffalo was involved in such a riot.

When the Civil War began, people flocked to service, volunteering in large numbers to serve the Union. Then, following the Battle of Bull Run and other Union losses, enthusiasm waned. An influx of opposition to the war ensued. A shortage of military manpower soon made it evident that the Union could lose the war unless something was done.

The first conscription act was passed in the spring of 1863. All male citizens between the ages of eighteen and thirty-five could be drafted to serve for three years. Many found disfavor with such medieval tactics of forcing service on a free people, but the issue chosen for protest became a class issue instead. A provision in the law stated that a man could either pay $300 or find someone to substitute in his place. How could a poor man afford the cost? Who would be willing to take someone else's place unless forced to do so? Some men formed clubs that pooled their funds to free at least one man from service if possible. Suddenly, patriotism was replaced by the slogan "The rich man's war and the poor man's fight." Furthermore, blacks could not be drafted; they were not considered citizens. Concern grew among immigrants that their jobs were threatened by the increasing numbers of blacks settling in Northern communities following Lincoln's Emancipation Proclamation.

Summer in Western New York is hot and sticky, sometimes leading to foul tempers and increased violent crime. July 1863 found the nation in the midst of a civil war, the city of Buffalo full of tension between immigrants and blacks and an unpopular draft quickly becoming a fuse in an open powder keg. New York State's governor, Horatio Seymour, believed that the president's unconstitutional proclamation would lead to dictatorship. When the conscription act was passed, Union agents went door to door throughout the region, seeking enrollees. This, too, was unconstitutional in that it violated a right to privacy, bordering on despotism. People were furious. The governor threw fuel on the fire following the Battle of Gettysburg by supporting these sentiments. Soon, immigrants, especially the Irish living and working on the waterfront, took up the cry, which became a roar on July 6 as a mob at the docks exploded into total chaos. All blacks within arm's reach were seized, attacked and beaten. At least two were killed. Rioters surrounded the Union Block as police forced their way through the throng.

The doors to Dug's Dive were seldom closed, and today was no exception. As the fighting threw itself along the canal district, some of it spilled from the towpath into Dug's saloon. Whenever the canal waters rose, the Dive, which was at water level, quickly flooded. Proprietor William Douglas always thought he would meet his end by drowning on one of those occasions, but today the flood was a human one, and he was spared. In the end, the police arrested as many blacks as they could, hauling them to jail for their own protection.

In only a matter of a day or two, things cooled in Buffalo. New York City would not be as fortunate.

Lincoln in Buffalo

By most accounts, Abraham Lincoln is considered one the country's greatest presidents. Buffalo has seen its fair share of presidential residents and visits, from the shooting of William McKinley during the Pan-American Exposition and Theodore Roosevelt taking his oath of office here to Buffalonians Millard Fillmore and Grover Cleveland. Yet nothing seems to equal the excitement and sorrow that Lincoln brought to the city.

As the gateway to the waterways and freedom, Buffalo hosted President Lincoln on his way to Washington D.C., to accept his presidency. Likewise, it played host briefly as Lincoln was carried home following his assassination.

It is fitting, perhaps, that this region should be a place that changed so many times and offered succor to the blacks as they experienced their great change too. It is also fitting that Buffalo should see Lincoln both as he entered and as he left his role in leadership of this great nation.

GIANTS IN WESTERN NEW YORK

STONE GIANTS

Among the Native Americans of Western New York, the Senecas and Tuscaroras, as well as natives of other regions, stone is considered a keeper of tales. Stone is the skeleton of the earth, having been around since the beginning of time. Stone has seen it all.

The native peoples also speak of Stone Giants, terrible beings that forgot their human ways, eat raw flesh and roll in earth and sand for their hard skin. These creatures came from the west. They were huge woodland beings similar to Bigfoot. Some say that they still roam the forested areas. Others say that ancient bones have been found. Whether they are still among us, Western New York has had other giants that left their imprints. They were the adventurous, the innovative, the fiery furnaces that fed the world during the industrial age.

When people need goods and demand is high, but they also desire low costs, entrepreneurs become creative. The Industrial Revolution rose from an increase in population. The age of machine was an age of mass production, communicative innovation and growth. Immigrants in great numbers labored in Buffalo's factories and mills to supply the nation. The skeletons of these giants can still be found in Western New York—from steel and grain mills to vacant factories and fond memories of days gone by. They are sometimes covered in cobwebs and rust, but there is no doubt that they were significant to both the region and the world.

FIRE-BREATHING GIANTS

Bethlehem and Lackawanna Steel breathed fire day and night to make the materials that built and moved a nation. From the bellies of these giants came steel for ships and rails, armor plating for the navy and designs in steel that made skyscrapers possible.

The village of Lackawanna, then a portion of West Seneca or Limestone Hill, was the perfect location for a steel operation, and Buffalo was the second-largest railroad center in the nation, with Lake Erie on the western edge. The Lackawanna Steel plant also boasted ten miles of rail track through its middle and sat near a large canal, with docks protected by a government break wall. These elements made it possible for this company to become a giant.

While Lackawanna Steel was born out of the Scranton Company of Pennsylvania, its influence gave the town of Lackawanna, New York, its name. Prior to 1909, the village of Lackawanna was part of West Seneca. After disputing who was responsible for funding improvements in the town, it was determined that the best way to solve the dilemma was to split the communities. The approximate area covered by the steel plant was, on average, over a half mile wide and three miles long. Company housing for its employees made up two villages located on its property. Later, during World War I, it also supplied a garden tract, where families grew what they needed. In addition, the company owned ore and coal mines in Pennsylvania, as well as elsewhere, making it a wealthy benefactor for the region.

Lackawanna Steel was considered "the greatest individual steel plant in the world." Ingenuity from this company helped to raise the battleship *Maine*, which sank in Havana, Cuba, in 1898. Steel sheet pilings designed and guaranteed by the company were selected by the Army Corps of Engineers in charge of the project, along with engineering plans from Lackawanna Steel.

Bethlehem Steel Company acquired Lackawanna Steel in 1922. The plant's furnaces continued to belch fire and smoke until 1982, when it closed its main division. Coke furnaces were operational until 2001, and a small galvanized steel plant employs a handful of workers. Nearby slag heaps now house eight giant windmills.

ELECTRIC GIANT

While George Westinghouse was not a Western New York native, he was an inventor who helped bring power for electricity and transportation to the region. His company was one of the greatest in the country, with worldwide impact. In 1896, in conjunction with Nikoli Tesla, this giant harnessed the mighty Niagara via hydroelectric power, lighting the city of Buffalo and revolutionizing delivery of electricity to places far from its source. In fact, Buffalo was twenty miles from the hydroelectric plant, remarkable for its day. Westinghouse also established a large manufacturing company in Western New York.

Where there is fire, there is smoke, and in the case of Western New York, there was also ice and water.

The electric chair, invented by Buffalo dentist Alfred Southwick, who is buried at Forest Lawn Cemetery.

ICE GIANT

Ancient Romans used the basic principles of air conditioning by circulating cool water via aqueducts throughout the walls of homes. Cisterns and wind towers were used by the Persians to cool environments. But it was Willis Haviland Carrier, a native of Angola, New York, who would bring cool air into our homes, hospitals and workplaces. Working for Buffalo Forge, Carrier designed heating and cooling systems for drying lumber and coffee in the early 1900s. When a Brooklyn printing firm had difficulty with its ink running, Carrier's work on cooling the air solved the problem, making three-color printing possible. Controlling the temperature and humidity of an environment made other manufacturing successful too. Carrier, who married three times, was buried, along with his wives, at Buffalo's Forest Lawn Cemetery.

WATER-SPOUTING, STEAM-BELLOWING GIANT

Born in Auburn, New York, Birdsill Holly employed over five hundred people at his Lockport plant. This giant gained world renown for putting out fires with his invention of the fire hydrant. Holly also created steam heating for homes and was important in the creation of the first steam-powered fire engine. A leader in hydraulic engineering, Birdsill Holly had over 150 patents. Every giant needs a cave, and the caves Holly Manufacturing used for water intake and discharge via the Erie Canal can still be toured by boat.

Giants are not always about fire, water and ice, however. Some have great arms that whisk away the water, some feed the masses and some can even fly.

WATER WHISKERS

Accidents will happen. On a rainy night in 1917, theatre manager John R. Oishei was driving down Delaware Avenue when his National Roadster collided with a bicycle. While the accident did not seriously injure anyone, it did set into motion that old adage "Necessity is the mother of invention." Greatly troubled by the incident, Oishei happened to see a sign in a shop window one day that belonged to a retired electrical engineer, John Jepson. The engineer had developed a tool that could be carried in an automobile's toolbox. When the weather turned inclement, the driver inserted it through the opening of a windshield and moved it back and forth. Oishei contracted with Jepson to manufacture his device as the "Rain Rubber." This was accomplished as a subsidiary of Stant Corporation, an early maker of automotive parts. By the end of World War I, Oishei had plants in Europe, Australia and North America, thereby changing the name of his subsidiary company to Tri-Continental Corporation, or Trico.

This giant's footprints go far beyond creating many wiper-blade products and becoming the largest independent employer in the city of Buffalo. John R. Oishei died in 1968 but left a continuing legacy for which many are grateful. The John R. Oishei Foundation continues to support many community endeavors, including medical research, academics and the arts. Western New York is richer because this giant chose to live and work here and to stay even after his death.

Granular Giants

Symbolic reminders of the industrial age, the skeletal remains of tall, granular giants continue to be a matter of contention in Western New York. These massive concrete structures occupying prime waterfront territory are unsightly to some but inspiring to others. In fact, innovative building designers from Europe once admired them.

Prior to 1827, grain traveled the heartland roads and waterways. Storms and poor road conditions delayed shipping. Cargo often arrived at its destination unusable due to spoilage. The opening of the Erie Canal, with its terminus at Buffalo and its proximity to the Great Lakes, made it the perfect place to develop new grain shipping techniques. This lowered the cost of shipping, making grain more profitable.

Lake ships could not traverse the narrow canal, so grain had to be reloaded into canalboats for shipment east. Most of the workers responsible for this labor were Irish immigrants. It was backbreaking, dangerous work because grain dust is highly combustible. Men working with it day and night contracted lung disease from breathing it in. Additionally, it took days to

Watson Grain Elevator, Buffalo Waterfront. This early wooden elevator had a slip directly underneath for canalboats to dock. Gravity loaded grain into the holds. *Courtesy of the Library of Congress Prints and Photographs Division.*

unload the ships, but that did not stop delivery into the Buffalo harbors. By the mid-1800s, bushels of grain and corn increased from approximately 100,000 to 2 million. Something had to be done to make it faster and less hazardous. In 1842, Joseph Dart, a Buffalo merchant, built the first grain elevator on the waterfront.

In this wooden structure that stored grain, Joseph incorporated a steam-powered conveyer with "buckets" attached to it. His invention lifted bucket after bucket full of raw grain from the hold of ships and dropped them into the structure's bins. Now the ships delivering grain to the harbor often arrived and left on the same day. This first elevator was to inspire others. By 1863, Buffalo had become the world's largest grain port, with twenty-seven elevators in its harbors.

Because they were fire hazards and prone to explosion, wooden elevators were eventually replaced by metal ones, with electrical elevators using Westinghouse motors. Later, these were replaced with concrete towers. Some of the world's leading giants in grain production settled here because of these technologies and the waterways. They included Pillsbury, General Mills and H.O. Oats. Cheerios, Wheaties and Gold Metal Flour continue to be produced here, but the Welland Canal in 1932 and the opening of the St. Lawrence Seaway brought the Western New York age of these giants to an end.

WHEELED GIANTS

Erwin Ross Thomas made a last-minute decision. Founder of the Thomas Motor Company in Buffalo, he would enter his 1907 Model 35 Thomas Flyer in the longest auto race in history: the New York–Paris automobile race of 1908.

Sponsored by the *New York Times* and *Le Matin* of Paris, the course would take the vehicles on a grueling twenty-two-thousand-mile journey. The cars were to ride on the railroad tracks when possible; if none were available, they traveled by road or muddy lanes and sometimes overland without roads. About 250,000 people cheered and waved as the race began on a February day in New York City. Six cars from four countries traveled west across the United States and China, through Siberia and Russia and on to Paris.

As the Thomas Flyer left the starting line, George Schuster, an employee of the motor company who was trusted for his mechanical skills, was at the

The New York–Paris Race. *Courtesy of the Library of Congress Prints and Photographs Division.*

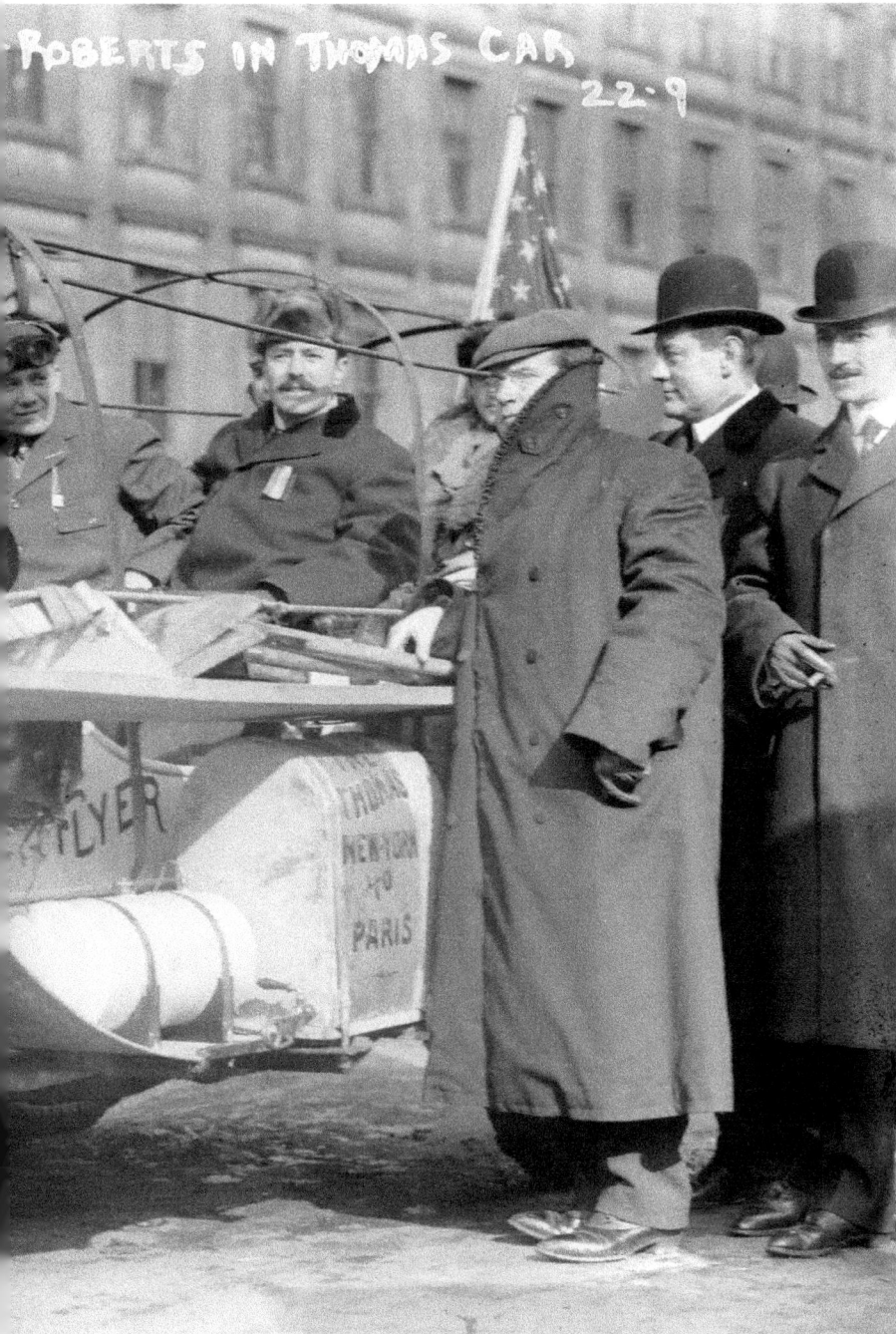

President Taft's Pierce-Arrow. *Courtesy of the Library of Congress Prints and Photographs Division.*

wheel. Throughout the race, a team of drivers took turns, much like a relay race. Schuster would be the only member to travel the whole distance. He also became the first person in history to drive across the United States in winter, a remarkable feat at a time when there were no snowplows, few roads, poor maps and no rest stops or roadside facilities.

When the cars reached the Pacific, they crossed by ship. The original plan had been to use the frozen Bering Strait, but they could not. In the end, only three cars completed the race. First place went to the vehicle made in Buffalo and driven by a Buffalo resident—George Schuster and the Thomas Flyer. What an incredible feat!

Another giant with wheels was George N. Pierce. What originally began as a business producing household items from iceboxes to gilded birdcages grew into a worldwide phenomenon. Although the company manufactured many commercial vehicles—fire trucks, camping trailers, motorcycles and bicycles—Pierce-Arrow Motor Car Company is best remembered for its first-class luxury automobiles. World greats proudly drove these cars. In 1909, President William Howard Taft ordered two. They were the first official automobiles of the White House. Many presidents after Taft would use Pierce-Arrow vehicles, and royals the world over ordered these fine autos.

They were status symbols for Hollywood movie stars and tycoons. David Jenkins, also called "Ab," broke world records on the salt flats of Utah in his 1932 Pierce-Arrow. However, a decline in sales brought on by the Great Depression and the creation of less costly vehicles caused the company to declare insolvency in 1938. Thus, another great Western New York giant became a ghostly specter of the past.

WINGED GIANTS

The giants with wings have flown in peace and wartime. Many planes and their various parts came from the skills and hard work of factory laborers in Western New York. Bell Aircraft, Calspan, Moog, Consolidated Aircraft, Curtiss-Wright, Irving Air Chute Inc. and Pratt & Whitney all looked to the skies, dared to dream and produced many world firsts and famous aerodynamic innovations. Bell Aircraft of Wheatfield produced the P-39 Aircobra; the X-1, first aircraft to break the sound barrier; the X-5, first swing-wing plane; the X-2, first to go past Mach 3; and the model 47 helicopter, used for medical evacuation in Korea. The region also put forth the first mass-produced parachutes, flying boats, the "Jenny" biplane and Calspan's transonic wind tunnel. Last, but certainly not least, the Curtiss-Wright P-40 was flown by the Flying Tigers in China.

Everyone thought that World War I would be the war to end all wars, yet in 1939, the Germans invaded Poland. It wasn't until December 7, 1941, that the United States entered World War II directly. Men, women and machines from all parts of the country lent themselves to the effort.

During World War I, women played supportive roles as telephone operators, performers and nurses. There were few opportunities outside of stereotypical women's work, but that changed dramatically during World War II. Buffalo's Curtiss-Wright, the world's largest aircraft manufacturer at the time, did not shy away from the desire of women to play a more active role. The company formed the Curtiss-Wright Cadettes, a program that sought top female math and science university students. These young women were trained as engineers and technicians to take the place of male workers when the country instituted the draft. Male employees who were not eligible for the draft continued to work for Curtiss-Wright, with women by their sides, some most likely taking part in assembling the P-40 fighter.

Curtiss P-40. The yellow-painted prop tips formed a circle as they spun.

Early P-40s went into production in 1929. Along with three other models being tested by Curtiss-Wright, the P-40 was flown secretly under the cover of darkness as a safeguard of patent. Few orders were placed for planes during the Great Depression. The company experienced a downturn that forced it to close some of its facilities. Glenn Curtiss, co-founder of the company, died in 1930 and never had the joy of knowing how his plane would win world fame.

Prior to the country's entry into the war, many P-40s were shipped to the British Air Force in North Africa. Their large radiators made them a favored aircraft for desert conditions. These planes engaged Japanese fighters during the attack on Pearl Harbor, fought the Germans and were flown in Africa by the first all-black fighter squadron.

Soldiers, sailors and "fly-boys" put their lives on the line and in the hands of those on the homefront daily. Men and women working in artillery, ammunition and tank, jeep and aircraft factories of the United States thought of the lives they might safeguard with their work. When the AVG (American Volunteer Group) in Burma, also called the Flying Tigers, took to the skies, Buffalo's P-40 planes were painted with shark's teeth on the nose and imbued with all the hopes of those who made them. The planes' reliability brought most of their pilots home safely.

Tasty Giant Bites

Some tigers may fly, but buffalos cannot. Yet they apparently have wings, or so many people worldwide have come to believe. You will find Buffalo wings on the menu in most places around the country, even around the world. Residents in the city of their origin do not call them Buffalo wings; they are simply known as wings. They breathe fire—hot, medium, mild and, for those with stone stomachs, suicide.

Travel around Buffalo and you will find more restaurants than you can visit in a year, even if you never went to the same one twice. It is the home of Beef on Weck, Wardynski's kielbasa, Sahlen's hotdogs, Weber's mustard and the best pizza and fish fries in the country. The southern tier counties were known for cheese making in the early days. There is actually a cheese museum in Cuba, New York. Of course, Buffalo is home to the chicken wing.

Established in 1935 by Frank and Teressa Bellissimo, the Anchor Bar on Main Street is the birthplace of this tasty international treat. The restaurant serves over one thousand pounds of wings per day and sends them worldwide by special order as well.

It all began one Friday night in 1964 when Teressa needed to feed late visiting friends of her son, Dominic. For the most part, the kitchen was closed and wiped down, with little left to make something from the regular menu. Teressa found some remainders from the day's supply of chicken. The wings hardly looked fitting to serve, so she mixed up a sauce, still a family secret, deep fried the wings and coated them in the sauce. What began as an experimental snack produced under poor circumstances became a phenomenon. People debate this legend and who in the world makes the best wings, but most agree that Anchor Bar is king. Teressa was a giant with a little idea that got a whole lot bigger than she expected. Today, Buffalo holds an annual wing festival large enough to fill a stadium.

Whether you like your wings mild, medium, hot or suicide, be sure to have a drink to wash them down. The region of Western New York has a long-standing history with beverage.

Western New York grape vineyards produce some of the finest wines and grape products in the world. Westfield, known as the "grape juice capital of the world" because of its location at the center of thirty thousand acres of vineyards, was once home to Welch's, the world leader in the manufacture of Concord and Niagara grape products. Many wineries are located in Chautauqua and Niagara Counties.

Buffalo was home to over thirty-five breweries in the 1800s. The largest (Palace Brewery) belonged to Gerhard Lang, an immigrant from Germany. Beer was big business during the Industrial Revolution and the heyday of the Erie Canal. By 1893, there were over two thousand saloons in Buffalo;

some say the city had a saloon on every corner. Eighty of them were owned by Lang. At that time, it was customary to drink beer in saloons rather than at home, so most were brewery owned. One of the most well-known breweries of the old days was Iroquois Brewery, which survived Prohibition by producing soda. Iroquois and William Simon were the last breweries in Buffalo, closing their doors in the early 1970s.

If a tamer beverage is desired, then Mayer Brothers cider might do the trick. Jacob Mayer began production in West Seneca in 1852. He opened a pressing mill for local growers. After his death, the operation passed to his son, John, who had a vision to do business year-round, where his father's business had been strictly at harvest time. John created new technology for juicing and bottling. Everyone in the region knows that it is autumn when these fine ciders appear in the marketplace.

Some giants still live here, such as Mentholatum, leader in manufacturing nonprescription drugs and healthcare products since 1889; Fisher Price Toys, which began here as a cottage industry and is now a subsidiary of Mattel; Rich Products, a world pioneer in frozen foods; and Sorrento, the largest seller of Italian cheese in the nation. But the industrial age is past. Most of the giants have either died or moved on, leaving footprints, skeletons and memories. A new time has come.

THE OSSIAN GIANT

Ossian is a small town in Livingston County and the early home of Frederick Decker, the Ossian Giant. Born on May 9, 1836, by the time Frederick was nineteen he stood seven feet, six inches in height, remarkable at a time when many people just pushed five feet. He weighed 385 pounds to boot!

Decker traveled to New York City, where he met P.T. Barnum, who at that time had a museum in the city. Impressed by Decker's stature, Barnum hired Frederick and renamed him the "Ossian Giant" after Decker's hometown. It may be that Barnum also gave some thought to the great Irish poet Ossian (Oisin), who wrote of the legendary giant Fionn mac Cumhaill.

The Ossian Giant performed with the likes of Tom Thumb. Able to hold over a dozen eggs in one hand, his big act was to hold a tiny woman in the palm of his hand. He spent several years with the circus and toured the country with its sideshow. After Barnum's New York City museum

The Ossian Giant, Frederick Decker, stands beside an average-sized man. *Courtesy of the Ossian Historical Society.*

burned, Ossian moved to Grove in Allegany County and retired from the national spotlight.

While Ossian did perform in some local town shows, as Frederick he had been a fine lumberjack prior to the circus and resumed that work in his retirement. He married an average-sized woman. Together, they had four average-sized children.

Upon his death on March 21, 1886, a custom-made coffin was loaded onto a sleigh by eight pallbearers and taken to the cemetery in Swain, New York. The Ossian Giant resides there now.

NATURAL WONDERS

THE TREES

Since the woodlands of Western New York were here when the first white men came in the 1600s, the region has a history of magnificent trees, and today's residents protect them whenever possible.

The oldest tree in the city of Buffalo, a fantastic three-hundred-year-old sycamore, shades Franklin Avenue. It contends with one other city tree as the oldest, that one being located in "the Meadows" at Delaware Park. Yet neither tree holds the title for "biggest east of the Rocky Mountains." That title goes to a tree that has long since left the region, the Giant Black Walnut Tree of Silver Creek.

The small town of Silver Creek is located south of Buffalo near the shores of Lake Erie. The black walnut stood there unmolested until it toppled in an 1822 storm. A Silver Creek merchant purchased the trunk and had it cut into sections. He preserved a portion by hollowing it out to use as an addition to his store. At over ten feet in diameter, it is said that a man once rode his horse through the tree and that it could accommodate twenty people. After a time, the tree section was sold, transported down the Erie Canal via Buffalo to New York City and then onward to London, England, where it was housed in a museum. Later, a fire in the museum destroyed it completely.

Another place with beautiful trees is Zoar Valley. Located between Silver Creek and Allegany State Park, it remains an exceptional example of old growth forest. The valley separates the counties of Cattaraugus and Erie by way of Cattaraugus Creek. Hauntingly beautiful, it has many wonderful trees and mossy hollows, including its ledge-clinging trees that hang out over the gorge by their roots.

Although many old trees can be found scattered throughout the region, they are understandably rare, as timber was a commodity used by the settlers for building their homes. Lumbering eventually became a local industry. In fact, in some places it was big business.

Settled in the early 1800s, Grand Island was home to thousands of fabulous white oak trees. Settlers built log homes on the island and cut the oaks for barrel staves. These staves were sent to Montreal and on to the West Indies to be made into barrels for molasses and rum. The Grand Island homesteaders were eventually removed by law because prominent Buffalo citizens complained to the governor about their lumbering operations, among other things. Years later, these same lands were sold to the East Boston Company, which intended to harvest the oaks for the shipyards of Boston and New York. They eventually cleared the land for a town.

The sawmill on the island at Whitehaven housed the largest steam-powered saw in the world. Many of the trees were up to five feet in diameter and seventy-five feet long. Once the majority of these magnificent trees were cut, the lumber company sold its holdings. Fortunately, today the residents of Grand Island have brought back the trees, and although not as ancient, the landscape is largely forested.

Just across the river from Grand Island, on the mainland, the town of Tonawanda became known as the "lumber city." Agriculture was a mainstay for the area, but once the Erie Canal opened, eastern lumber buyers took a real interest in the timber available from parts west, such as Michigan, Wisconsin, Minnesota and even Ontario, Canada. Tonawanda handled its first shipment of lumber in 1867.

Home to the Fancher Chair Company, one of the oldest manufacturing companies, dating to 1807, the southern region had smaller sawmills scattered wherever creeks were available for shipping and power. Cold Spring in Cattaraugus County boasted pines that stood two hundred feet tall. Also relying on the wealth of the region's timber were Poland, Jamestown, Carroll, Harmony and Sherman in Chautauqua County, along with South Valley, Carrolton and most of Allegany County.

In the 1930s, Dutch elm disease from Europe ravaged Western New York elms. Then, on October 12, 2006, many area residents were stunned by a fierce snowstorm at a time when the leaves were still on most trees. Leaf-laden branches became heavy with snow. People going to bed that night could

Sycamore tree, oldest tree in Buffalo. This tree is located on Franklin Street. *Courtesy of the author.*

never have imagined the destruction that awaited them the next morning. A community that adores its trees, and indeed is known for them, woke to find tens of thousands of trees broken or uprooted and many damaged beyond saving. This storm broke the hearts of many residents, who wept openly at the loss. The good news is that many trees did survive and are once again beautiful. They are changed, much like the region itself, but the old sycamore still lives, reminding us of our rich history.

The Eternal Flame

Western New Yorkers take pride in preserving wildlife, trees and open lands. The region is rich in parks and recreational areas, including Letchworth State Park in Monroe/Livingston County and Chestnut Ridge Park in Erie County, both built by the Civilian Conservation Corp and the Works Progress Administration during the Great Depression. Appropriately, the shelters at Chestnut Ridge are made of timber from American chestnut trees that were dying of disease. Located in the park is a deep glen carved by Shale Creek. It is the sanctuary of the eternal flame.

Chestnut Ridge is expansive, but visitors following Shale Creek will come to a thirty-foot waterfall, where, over time, the cascading water carved a small grotto. A veil of water shrouds the grotto, and behind it is an eternal flame. Sometimes it does go out, but someone always relights it, allowing the next visitor to have that same experience as the early settlers.

One can imagine what it was like for an early settler exploring the region. Trekking long distances through the thick tree and brush cover of the Chestnut Ridge wilderness, he followed the sound of rushing water until he came to a creek. The traveler climbed down the steep ravine in order to fill his canteen and then followed that creek because it was the easiest way to travel such dense woods. As he approached a waterfall, he caught his breath at the sight before him: the water was on fire.

The southern region of Western New York is rich in natural gas deposits. Natural gas is produced when ancient decaying materials seep through the cracks and pores in shale. It is prevalent in this region, including in Chestnut Ridge Park. Chautauqua, Cattaraugus and Allegany Counties hold many large gas reservoirs. Genesee County is also rich in natural gas, as well as gypsum, limestone and salt. Early settlers found pockets of this gas bubbling up in the their ponds and streams and put it use. The stone lighthouse at

The eternal flame in its natural alcove at Chestnut Ridge Park. Trail makers are found off Seufert Road in Orchard Park, New York. *Courtesy of the author.*

Barcelona, New York, was the first worldwide to be powered by natural gas and the first public building in the United States to use this resource. Fredonia boasted the nation's first natural gas well, drilled in 1821, and the first natural gas lighting company.

Silencing Niagara

Since long before man came to the region, the mighty Niagara and its falls have thundered as a reminder that there are powers greater than our own. People have relied on the river for sustenance and travel and, later, to power industry and for tourism. One can almost get used to the noise of the cascade and the movement of the currents, but it is impossible to forget that these waters are why we settled here. Although he has reverence for the water's majesty, man has used the river and the falls for his own purposes. It has been harnessed for power, ridden for fame, given sacrifice and slowed for conservation. Twice it was temporarily halted, but the mighty Niagara has never been conquered.

Comprising three separate cascades, Niagara Falls was divided between Canada and the United States in the Treaty of Paris following the Revolutionary War. The Rainbow Falls and Luna Falls, also known as the Bridal Veil, are American; the Horseshoe Falls are in Canada. The falls are a perfect metaphor for the two countries that are separated and different but come from the same source. Popular among honeymooners, the falls are symbols of endurance. Interestingly, the first recorded honeymoon at Niagara Falls was when Napoleon Bonaparte's brother, Jerome, brought his American bride there in 1804.

During tourist season, 100,000 cubic feet of water per second pour over the falls each day. Since the hydroelectric plants were built, it has been possible to cut this flow in half during the non-tourist season. This is done for conservation and to allow more water to the intakes for power without harming the effect that draws millions of visitors from all over the world. Fittingly, this is a joint effort by Canada and the United States. The waters of the Horseshoe Falls were slowed to a trickle intentionally in 1953 to allow conservation work. For beautification by rock removal, the American Falls were stopped in 1969, although it was soon determined that the rocks could not be removed after all. Man just doesn't seem to give up trying to manipulate these waters, always forgetting their power, even in winter, when shallow Lake Erie freezes.

The ice of Lake Erie has been used for travel and recreation for centuries, but people often underestimate its danger. Ice fishermen build shanties, and people take walks on the ice, sometimes becoming stranded. Approximately 150 fishermen had to be rescued on February 9, 2009, when the ice beneath them cracked and separated. One man died.

Unlike the lake, the Niagara River flows too swiftly to freeze. Still, large ice floes from the lake can damage property and cause problems with the intakes at the electric plants. Because of this, each season since 1964, an ice boom is put in place to hold back the floes. It is rare when Mother Nature does this without man's help, but it has happened. Before the ice boom was utilized, there were several times when Mother Nature stopped both the American Falls and the Horseshoe Falls.

On four occasions from 1909 to 1949, the American Falls froze after becoming jammed by ice buildup. Many people took advantage of the phenomenon and walked on the ice. But there is only one time in recorded history that nature has stopped the Horseshoe Falls. On that occasion, people thought the world had come to an end, yet they were curious, too.

MARCH 29, 1848

A gale-force wind blew in off Lake Erie. During the night, huge slabs of ice moved ominously in the darkness, one after the other pushed upright until none could move. Many mills upriver of the falls used the swift currents to turn their machinery, and on that day they ceased to function. Millers were roused early from their beds to be told by their workers that their raceways had gone dry.

"There are fish floundering on the dry riverbed," their workers said with a measure of fear.

One can only imagine the reply. "Nonsense," the miller might have said, thinking to himself that his lazy employee was making excuses to get out of the day's work. "It's the Niagara! How could it be stopped?"

But it was. People so used to hearing the constant roar of the falls were shocked into wakefulness by absolute silence. Only a small trickle of water dripped over the 170-foot precipice. Jagged rocks below the falls were exposed, and fish lay there flopping about, along with a wealth of artifacts from days gone by. Debris and many items from the War of 1812 lay scattered. That Sunday, churches filled with people who thought the world was ending, including some who had not attended in a long time. Many prayed for salvation. Others thought, Why not take a little stroll, or better, harness up the horse and buggy? People walked and drove out into the barren riverbed at the precipice; a squad of soldiers rode in exhibition. On the night of March 31, the whole spectacle came to an end as shifting winds broke apart the ice. Beginning as a low groan from upriver, a wall of water suddenly raced forward. The Niagara has never again been silenced.

WHISTLING WELL

Wind, barometric pressure and current changes herald storms. A sailor's life on the Great Lakes depends on this knowledge. A lake storm can easily capsize even a fairly large boat. Schooners one hundred feet or more in length have gone aground, or worse, in such storms. A good sailor keeps an eye on the skies, relying on tools such as the barometer.

In Cattaraugus County, many miles from the lake, there is a natural barometer at Great Valley. The Whistling Well, or Breathing Well, as it is sometimes called, was located on the farm of Nicholas Flint. Like most settlers who built away from lakes and rivers, Nicholas needed to dig his own well. He dug to twenty-five or more feet but did not find water. Instead, a steady stream of air emanated from its depths. He capped the well with a slab that had a hole drilled in it and then inserted a whistle in the hole. When air pressure changed before a storm, the whistle blew as air was forced upward from the well. The sound was heard over a mile away. In fair weather, air was taken into the well and all was silent.

Several scientists traveled to Great Valley to see the well but could not figure out what made the air currents below. They presumed there was a subterranean source. Today, the whistle is gone and the hole is capped. Little air moves in the chamber because it has filled with debris. But the whistling well remains a local legend.

MURDER, MAYHEM AND MORE

A HANGING IN LAFAYETTE SQUARE

Frontier justice changed when the wilderness was settled. Laws and punishments became centralized under the already established United States legal system. This system, established by the Constitution, afforded each citizen a proper trial by peers and imprisonment only with justification. Prior to that, a lawbreaker was lucky to make it to town, let alone to trial. As the largest city in Western New York, Buffalo was the seat of government, with a courthouse, a jail and a public commons located in Lafayette Square.

Named for General Lafayette, who visited Buffalo in 1825, it was here that scaffolds were built for hangings. Not unlike in other cities, Buffalo citizens gathered for executions; they were social events and an important part of the system. People attending an execution were witnesses to justice. The first murder trial in Erie County was held in 1815, but perhaps one of the best known was the Thayer trial in the spring of 1825.

Nelson, Isaac and Israel Jr. Thayer climbed the gallows' stairs. They looked neither left nor right and spoke not a word, not even to one another. They did not struggle or resist along the march or as the nooses were placed over their heads. The Reverends Fillmore and Story ended their prayers, "May God have mercy on your souls, amen." Each brother thanked the preachers, briefly clasped hands and wished farewell to assembled friends and officers. Their hands were tied and the ropes adjusted. Wade S. Littlefield, sheriff, raised the Sword of Justice, gave it a steady swing and cut the rope that dropped the gallows' floor. A din rose from the thousands of onlookers, and then all fell silent.

One wonders at the calmness of the Thayers on the day they met their maker. Perhaps they accepted justice for their foul deed as readily as they might have accepted reward for a good deed, or perhaps they had little thought or care. Reports say that they showed no remorse, joking and laughing until the very day of their hanging.

The Thayer farm was more than a day or two's ride from the city, in the wilderness where men often took the law into their own hands. Who would know if someone were to suddenly disappear and not be seen again?

With only an aging father at home, the brothers were known to be crude. They clung to old ways in the manner of their dress, used foul language and were boastful. They drank too much and brutalized one another and their oxen, which were named Almighty God and Jesus Christ. With this lack of supervision and their wilderness mindset, they never imagined that they would be caught for the murder they committed. Poor as they were, they may have felt justified. After all, the man they killed had more than his fair share.

It all began with a sailor and peddler named John Love. No records exist saying what John Love sold or exactly how he traveled, except that he owned a horse. Unfortunately for Love, one day his path crossed the Thayer farm.

It may have been late in the day and he was concerned about traveling unknown territory in the dark, or he might have found this a convenient place from which to base his operations with locals. Regardless, John Love became a boarder, taking up residence with the Thayers when he was not off someplace else. He had money to spare; in fact, he had enough money to warrant loaning it from time to time. Why, even Isaac, the youngest Thayer brother, had borrowed money from Love, yet the Thayers apparently were not satisfied by what he gave them. Likely a time came when Love asked for repayment of the loans. When John Love suddenly stopped visiting neighboring farms to hawk his wares, and the Thayers found themselves in possession of a very nice horse and extra spending money, people became suspicious. It didn't help their case when one of the boys had the "bright" idea to collect on Love's other debts. When Isaac Thayer showed up in Buffalo, he was taken into custody.

When questioned, Isaac said that Love had loaned them the horse while he was away in Canada. But with a ten-dollar reward for the recovery of John Love's body, it didn't take long for someone to find it. The district attorney, General Potter, confronted Isaac.

John Love's grave marker at Maplewood Cemetery in Boston, New York. *Courtesy of the author.*

"Well, Mr. Thayer, the body of John Love has just been found in a gully near your father's house. The man was shot and buried in a shallow grave with a blanket over his head. What have you to say for yourself?"

Thayer could say little, and his father and two brothers soon joined him in the old stone jail.

John Love had been murdered in December 1824. The trial took place in the Buffalo courthouse on April 21–23, 1825, with the Honorable Reuben H. Walworth presiding. Evidence was so supportive that the jury returned a verdict of guilty within thirty minutes. The brothers confessed to the murder, saying they had been threatened by Love's business tactics. He had taken possession of most of their property in payment, and they had not been able to deal peacefully with him. But the law is the law. Someone was murdered, and justice would be served. Aged and in ill health, Israel Sr. was released, but his sons, ages twenty-one to twenty-five, were sentenced to death by hanging.

On June 7, 1825, a military parade of militia, a horse troop, artillery and a rifle company formed on Washington Street across from the jail. The prisoners would not escape. The door to the old jail opened, and Sheriff Littlefield led the procession, holding before him the Sword of Justice, a symbol entrusted to his office. Under heavy guard, the prisoners descended the steep staircase to the street below. The Thayers wore white caps and shrouds as they walked behind the wagon that bore their coffins. No longer able to laugh and joke, the brothers summoned all their courage just to stand upright. A band played a slow, rhythmic funeral dirge as the brothers walked between the rows of guards and soldiers. Just beyond the guard, they could see the gaping crowds. As the procession rounded the corner onto Court Street, no doubt they could also see the shadow of the scaffold that rose before them in the square. Reality set in as their final moments on earth lay before them.

John Love's death was avenged by justice. Within thirty minutes from the time Sheriff Littlefield swung the sword, the first trio to be executed together were coffined and on their way home for burial in Boston, New York.

The actual location of this hanging is disputed in various reports, some referring to Niagara versus Lafayette Square. Regardless, the hanging took place and was not soon to be forgotten.

Treasure of Panama Rocks

Inhabited by Mound Builders, the Eriez Indians, and traveled by early French explorers, the area known today as Panama, New York, was permanently settled in 1810. It was named by Panama Joe, who once visited the Isthmus of Panama. The rocks here reminded him of it, so he called the region Panama.

Located in Chautauqua County near the Pennsylvania border, Panama Rocks Park has the largest deposit of glacier-cut ocean quartz in the world, with a ridge extending about a half mile. Covered now by forest, this was once an ocean bed. The gigantic rock formations, pushed forward by the glaciers, are a delight to explore. There are many caves, passages and dangerous crevices within the rocks. These crevices once hid treasure; some say they still do.

In the early 1800s, a courier carrying gold was waylaid on his way to Clymer. He must have been traveling from the east, or perhaps from Jamestown, as Panama would have been along this line. With few, if any, real roads, the courier had to ride through thick woods and rocky terrain, making him an easy target. Robbers leapt on him as he passed, stole his cargo and made good their escape before he could recover his wits. Not knowing the area as readily as the robbers, he could not pursue them, but he made his report when he arrived at his destination.

The robbers certainly knew that the courier would report the heist, so they dared not be seen by day. Waiting until nightfall, the men wove their way among the great rocks, lowered their loot into a hole and planned to return when the "heat was off." These rocks are both beautiful and treacherous. When the robbers finally returned to retrieve their booty, they could not remember into which hole they had dropped it. It was never found.

A few years later, a ring of counterfeiters was said to have used the rocks as a hideout for their operations. They minted on the spot, hiding both their dies and their coins. After a full day's work "making" their living, the gang retired to a nearby inn. Local legend says that when the inn burned, thousands of dollars in counterfeit coins were found in the rubble, along with a secret passageway leading from the inn to their rock hideout.

Yet another robber's tale is connected with Chautauqua Creek, which empties into Lake Erie. Sometime around 1735, French trappers, returning from a successful trade with gold in their satchels, were attacked by Indians. Hemmed in on a ledge, the trappers found a cave and in it buried their valuables, including the gold coins. When nightfall came, they were able to escape the Indians. Later, when it was safe, the trappers returned, hoping to retrieve their belongings, but they never found the cave again.

More than the beauty of rocks and trees are found in these lovely places. Watch where you walk and perhaps there will be a glimmer of gold, or it may be just a legend playing tricks on the brain.

ARARAT, CLINTON'S DITCH AND THE MYSTERY OF WILLIAM MORGAN

OCTOBER 1827

A body washes ashore near Fort Niagara. A pale-faced woman stands supported by one of the coroner's arms as he pulls back the sheet with the other.

"Do you recognize this man?" he asks.

She lets out a long, hollow sob. "Yes, he is my husband."

Mrs. William Morgan identified the dead man as her missing husband, William. Her life would be forever changed, as would the existence of the Country Grand Lodge of the Freemasons, but at least she now knew what had become of him. Or did she?

Thurlow Weed, a political powerhouse and member of the Masons, had been accused of shaving the face and head of the corpse to make it look more like William Morgan, although this was never substantiated. However, on his own deathbed in 1882, Weed admitted to the murder of William Morgan. He claimed that he and five other men had abducted Morgan, bound him in chains and dumped him into the river. He accused John Whitney of having been one of the five men.

To this very day, the facts in this case remain uncertain. Whitney's confession, separate from that of Weed's, seems a more likely story, but even that is lacking in evidence. Whitney's version of the story has Morgan accepting a bribe and being whisked away to Canada and then, via ship, to parts unknown, never to be seen again. One thing we do know for sure is that William Morgan was never seen alive in Western New York again.

For those uninitiated into its rites, the unknown origins and secrecy of Freemasonry caused much fear. Freemasonry was on the verge of collapse due to anti-Masonic sentiments, which the events of William Morgan's death only served to strengthen. At the same time, Western New York was poised for huge changes that would usher in the industrial age in the region, forever putting the city of Buffalo on the map.

Mordecai M. Noah, born in 1785 in Philadelphia, was known to have ties to the Jewish Masons in Charleston. He became a Freemason before age twenty-one, but instead of joining the Charleston Masons, he joined a rival order of the York Rite. By 1818, Mordecai was a Royal Arch Mason.

Active in politics, Mordecai backed Democrat Martin Van Buren, a major opponent to New York City mayor Dewitt Clinton. Clinton and Daniel Thomkins, one-time governor of New York and vice president for James Monroe, played important roles in Mordecai Noah's future plans. Mordecai was in a tangled web with Thomkins and Clinton, his superiors in the Masons but also his political enemies because he supported Van Buren.

Unsuccessful in his race for president in 1812, Mayor Dewitt Clinton, "the Father of the Erie Canal," put all of his effort into making sure the "Ditch" got dug. But when Thomkins became vice president under Monroe, relinquishing his role as governor of New York, Clinton ran as the only candidate for governor and won in 1816. That same year, he became "High Priest" for the Royal Arch Masons of the United States. He won a second term as governor, all the while keeping his post as president of the Erie Canal Commission. In 1824, Van Buren's "Bucktails," enemies to Clinton, tried to remove him from the commission. Consequently, although not renominated for governor, this angered enough people that Clinton was reelected and served two additional terms. He never gave up his desire to see the canal to completion. Mordecai Noah supported these efforts, even though he was a Van Buren man. It was no surprise either that Clinton, a Mason, one-time mayor of the city at the other end of the canal and now governor of the state, had such an interest in the canal project.

This story is full of political intrigue. Noah backed both Van Buren and Clinton, who hated each other. But there had to be more to it. Mordecai was no fool; he had a plan of his own and used them both to fulfill it. In 1818, Noah called on all Jews to form a new Jewish homeland. For Noah, that homeland was to be Grand Island, New York, newly acquired by the Treaty of Ghent. He attempted to convince the state legislature to give him ownership in 1820. He apparently thought that his political ties would hold, but even with support from the New York City Jewish community, his bid failed. Yet Noah was not giving up. He found several backers to help him purchase much of the land on Grand Island. Now, he and his associates held title. All of this maneuvering on Noah's part took place simultaneously with the Bucktails keeping Clinton busy with issues over the canal and the governor's race. In 1825, Noah appointed himself head of the restored Jewish government and asked for annual "tribute" in silver from all Jews worldwide.

So we have Thomkins and Clinton, both high-ranking political officials and Masons, and Mordecai Noah, who knew how to get what he wanted, backing political opponents to do so. We also have one dead or missing William Morgan. This begs the question: who's minding the store? Due to a division among the New York Masons in 1823, the Western New York Mason's lodges were growing in number, and they looked forward to future growth in the region. This just happened to coincide with not only Noah's bid for Grand Island but also Clinton's westward push for the canal. At the same time, New York City Masonic leaders did not want to give much power to these lodges because they disagreed with the split in the first place. Western New York lodges were not happy with this lack of power. There was an open revolt, and the regional "Country Lodge" was formed. With all of this bickering, nobody was really in charge of the region's Masons.

A rift had formed in a powerful organization with deep historical roots. If one were a conspiracy theorist, one might even blame powerful leaders such as Clinton, Thomkins and even Noah for allowing things to get so frayed. Of course, none of this looked good to a public that was already suspicious of the Freemasons. Everything pointed to trouble. Enter William Morgan.

Captain William Morgan, a War of 1812 veteran and brick mason, lived with his wife in Batavia, New York, from 1824 to 1826. He has been described as a ne'er-do-well, careless with his money but cunning. He eventually made rank of Royal Arch in the Leroy, New York lodge in 1825, but according to records, his name never even appears as having joined the Masons. This gives one pause to wonder if he was a liar, a wannabe, a spy sent to dig up dirt on the local Masons or perhaps simply an opportunist. He signed a petition to make the Leroy lodge official, but his name was stricken from the list, so maybe he was angry about that. Nevertheless, he took part in local Freemasonry and, in 1826, contracted with three men to publish a book. One of these men had been hindered from advancement in the Masons, and a second was Morgan's landlord. Little is known of the third man. The book deal promised Morgan a lot of money, and he bragged about it. The book? It promised to tell the secrets of Royal Arch rites and expose corruption in the Country Lodge.

The more Morgan bragged, the less kindness was shown to him, until eventually he was arrested on trumped-up charges for stealing a shirt and tie. He was acquitted and then immediately arrested again for a debt of only a

A Freemason membership certificate. *Courtesy of the Library of Congress Prints and Photographs Division.*

few dollars and cents. Released when an unknown benefactor paid his debt, Morgan was taken by several men via coach to an unused powder magazine at Fort Niagara. That was the last time he was seen alive. Governor Clinton issued a reward for his whereabouts, promising punishment to any who harmed him, but Morgan's body was not found—at least not until that day his wife identified him. By then, there was no hope of finding the culprits.

William Morgan's book, *Masonic Secrets Revealed*, was published after his disappearance and became a bestseller. Intended originally to expose the Royal Arch specifically, it was actually printed as secrets of the Blue Lodge rituals. As a result of his demise, a series of protests against the Masons followed. The organization fell under strong criticism, and the Country Lodge was disbanded. One of its leaders, Stephen Van Rensselaer, took leadership of a newly formed conglomerate. An anti-Masonic political party was formed. Noah Mordecai's plan for Grand Island failed as a result of Morgan's disappearance. Widow Morgan became one of the many wives of Latter Day Saints founder Joseph Smith. As a result, William Morgan was given one of the first official "Baptisms for the Dead" in the Mormon Church. His monument stands in the Batavia Cemetery.

Three separate inquests were held about the body that was found. The first favored Mrs. Morgan's identification. In the third, Mrs. Sara Monroe of Canada claimed that the man was her husband, Timothy Monroe. The court accepted this identification; the body belonged to Monroe, not Morgan. Then, in June 1881, another body was uncovered in a quarry at Pembroke, not very far from Batavia. A crumpled piece of paper was found in a metal box with the body. It hinted that this was William Morgan.

Was he dead or alive in 1826? Perhaps he was sitting in a Paris café, counting book proceeds, enjoying a fine wine and thinking to himself, "It worked."

KILLER IN THE STREET AND A POTTERS' FIELD

Death walked the streets of Buffalo looking for its next victim. By the time this killer was finished, hundreds were hastily buried. The three thousand victims in Montreal and Quebec had not been enough, nor were any of the others from New York City to Albany and all of the towns along the Erie Canal. This killer needed watery places to live and humans to carry it; it robbed the body of all salts and fluids and then replicated itself. Cholera could not be satiated.

In the summer of 1832, not too long after the first death in Albany, cholera paid its first visit to Buffalo. On July 16, an Irishman became ill. He was the first, and he died within eight hours.

Brought over from Europe by immigrants, cholera rode the canalboats to Buffalo. It struck the weakest citizens first and then seemingly healthy men. Stricken by nightfall, they were dead by morning's light. Traffic on the canal and coach lines came to a near standstill as fear gripped the city and towns. "You can't stop here. Move on." became a familiar mantra at canal ports and coach stops. Cart drivers called from the street, "Bring out your dead!"

Canal warehouses, factories and poorhouses became makeshift hospitals. Food grew scarce as local farmers refused to travel into the city with produce for fear of becoming infected. Many residents fled, in some cases unknowingly taking the disease with them. Some stopped drinking alcohol, as they thought the disease only killed drunkards. Some wore wooden shoes, believing the soil was tainted. The smell of rotting meat hanging on poles, burning tar and lime hung in the air. It was believed that these would stop the spread of the killer disease. Yet flies and insects attracted to the rotting meat and waterways settled on human waste and landed on food meant for human consumption—the true way the disease was spread.

Almost as quickly as death had come with the summer, it left with the fall. The canal once again bustled with activity as boat captains tried desperately to gain ground before winter froze them out. But cholera was not yet finished. It returned again in 1834, 1849 and 1854, each time causing fear. In 1849, over nine hundred people in the region died.

Perhaps because of the population bases and easy travel along the canal, New York State was among the hardest hit by the cholera epidemic, a disease that moves rapidly through the human body. While indiscriminate, the disease did strike the working class first, likely because of exposure on the canal front and poorer sanitary conditions. Many travelers on the canalboats fell ill for the same reason.

Yes there were heroes who came to the forefront, as they always do when things get tough in Western New York. Doctors and nurses tended the sick, ministers and sextons cared for the dying and dead and Roswell Haskins, an everyday man and printer by trade, carried sick people from tenement buildings on his back, refusing death its due. Many died in the city but could not be buried there. Any dead of a disease such as cholera had to be immediately removed from the city proper to a rural burying ground. Buffalo's potters' field was the place for most of them.

The site of City Honors School, the old potters' field, was a disorganized burial plot outside the city limit. Once rural, this type of burial ground was common worldwide throughout history. Sometimes called "stranger's cemeteries," they were usually reserved for unknown dead and indigents. When the epidemic of 1832 became evident, William Hodge, who had purchased a lot for farming from the Holland Land Company, sold the five acres between current-day Best and North Streets to the city for a common burial site. A portion of this acreage was set aside for Catholic burial. In 1886, no longer in use as intended, the graves were moved to the newly formed Forest Lawn Cemetery, the afterlife home to many world-famous people. The former burial ground became one of Frederick Law Olmsted's many parks, Masten Park. Later, in 1897, it became the site of Masten Park High School, now City Honors School.

When workmen began digging for the school's foundation in 1895, they found at least twenty-five skeletons. As late as 2007, archaeologists hired to oversee new construction of the high school due to its past history uncovered an additional 125 graves. Because many of the dead buried in the old burial grounds were poor or rapidly interred to avoid contagion, many were not recorded and their graves were unmarked. Some of the unearthed graves were empty; clearly, some had been desecrated. But these newly discovered bodies were able to join the others at Forest Lawn by agreement.

Today, the potters' field is a highly respected city school, the Erie Canal is used for recreation and cholera is a forgotten nightmare.

Gasport Burns

Gasport, New York, is a small hamlet in the town of Royalton, located on the Erie Canal. As with many small towns and villages from Albany to Buffalo, it owes its existence to the canal. In fact, when the Erie Canal ceased to function as a major thoroughfare for shipping, many of these small towns dwindled in population.

The hamlet of Gasport gets its name from the natural gas deposits once found there. Ironically, a community that could create fire from a natural source was one of two that did not adopt Birdsill Holly's fire protection system, the fire hydrant. The other was Chicago. Both burned, but remarkably, the Gasport fire occurred just hours after Mr. Birdsill Holly, a mysterious man in his own right, died on April 27, 1894.

THE FILLMORE GANG

Right out of an old western movie, Western New York is no stranger to horse thievery. In the Old West, one could be hanged on the spot for such dastardly deeds as stealing a man's rifle or horse, two things relied on for survival. But prison was the sentence for conviction of lesser crimes in this region in the 1800s, and the Fillmore gang heard the resounding clang of prison bars.

John Allen looked side to side before entering Red Tavern. Nothing was out of the ordinary—no sheriff, nothing suspicious. Inside, Henry Hyslip, Jerry Whaley and Tyler waited.

"What's taking him so long?" Tyler asked, nervous as usual.

"He'll be here," Henry replied.

Jerry nodded in confirmation toward the door. "Here now."

The other two men turned their heads. "Okay, John?"

"Okay," he answered.

The four men had just returned from another good night of horse stealing on the Buffalo Reservation.

"Nothin's easier than borrowing horses from the Injuns," he added.

But John Allen was wrong. While they had been at it for a while, with their hideout at the mouth of Cold Creek and Ed Rice, proprietor of the tavern,

Trial of a Horse Thief. Courtesy of the Library of Congress Prints and Photographs Division.

looking the other way anytime they showed up, the law was on to them. The four leaders of the gang were arrested, found guilty and sent off to prison with a few other members. That ended the gang from Fillmore for good.

The One Who Got Away

After putting on his high boots, Charles Churchill picked up the pitchfork and headed for the stable. He took a deep breath of fresh morning air before entering to muck the stalls. Opening the door, he stepped inside, anticipating the usual friendly whinny of his latest bay mare. He was met with silence. She was gone!

The door had been closed, he was sure of that. There was no sign of the stall being kicked in. The halter was missing. "Horse thieves," he said under his breath as he rushed to saddle up his older horse.

Churchill's horse was just the latest in a string of horse thefts that plagued the region in the year 1890. When Churchill reached the town of Patchin, word spread quickly. The vigilante committee of elected officers and sworn deputies formed at the tavern.

"You're not alone Charles," said one of the other men. "Jake here and Sirus, and a couple others, have had horses stolen. It's time to do something about it, and we think we know who the man is. It's only a matter of time before we catch him, don't you worry."

That had been in the fall, and try as they could, the committee was unable to find the culprit's trail, until one day in midwinter when a missing horse's tracks took them right to the thief. He was apprehended in Colden, just east of Patchin. The sun had already begun to set as the sheriff and his deputies zeroed in on their quarry. Once they had him, there was no sense in moving farther that night, as the Buffalo jail was too far to travel, so they laid up in the hotel. The thief was locked in a second-story room without any clothes; those were in the sheriff's possession as a safeguard. No man would be foolish enough to run bare naked on a Western New York winter's night, now would he?

Morning revealed the bedsheets tied to a bedpost, hanging out the window into a snowdrift. The accused was gone, along with the horse. They chased that man throughout the countryside, through Holland and South Wales, until the trail went cold. Finally, the sheriff and his men followed a lead that took them to the thief's house in East Aurora. He must have used a blanket from the bed to cover himself against the cold because they found it tucked away in the barn. Watching the house for two days from a distance, they finally saw him ride in with a store of food. The thief caught wind of them and ran again. After hunting him down from one place to the next, it was finally decided to put out a fifty dollar reward, but even that proved fruitless. He was the horse thief who got away.

LAKE ERIE SERPENT

Since the earliest days of sailing, seamen have spotted creatures of the deep. Many myths were told that frightened potential sailors and explorers so that they marked these terrible demons on ancient world maps as a warning. Lake Erie also has its sea monster, or giant serpent, fondly named Bessie.

Sightings of a large beast in the lake are recorded as early as 1817. In a paper written by Charles G. Olmstead Esq., of Buffalo, we are told that on the third of July, just thirty miles from Buffalo, the crew on the schooner *General Scott* saw a serpent forty feet in length, its head twelve inches in diameter. Bessie, as she became known, was dark mahogany in color and remained in sight for more than a minute on calm waters.

Bessie continued to be seen off and on for a few decades following the sighting by the *General Scott* crew. People have occasionally reported seeing something unexplainable right through the 1900s. Yet Bessie is not the only serpent seen in inland waters. In the early 1800s, after a particularly heavy storm, a serpent was spotted in the Mohawk Valley. Since the Erie Canal was not completed until 1825, does this mean there is a second family of serpents out there? One has to wonder, even though no sightings have been made in a long time, whether the canal locks will keep them from migrating.

LAND OF SPIRITS AND THE BURNED-OVER DISTRICT

Western New York definitely has a spiritual aura, with hundreds of beautiful churches and synagogues ranging from Gothic and Romanesque to ornate or simply modern. Niagara Falls, sacred to ancient native peoples, continues its powerful hold over the region. In the southern counties, one finds shaded glens reminiscent of those sacred places in Ireland and old growth forests that haunt us from the past.

Something moves throughout Western New York that touches us.

LEY LINES AND QUARTZ VORTEXES

Ley lines are unseen lines of sight or energy, depending on your personal beliefs. Some say that all major megaliths, including Stonehenge, are located on ley lines. It is believed that they are like points on a survey, indicating the quickest way to travel from point A to point B. Others say that they are lines that follow the earth's energy.

Do ley lines run through Western New York? Proponents say that Hill Fort Cemetery in Auburn, New York (not part of Western New York), is located on a ley line. This ancient hilltop fortification belonged to Mound Builders. Similar sites within Western New York have yielded many artifacts. Though these mounds are not as large, Mound Builders were here long before the Eriez and the Iroquois.

It is said that ley lines crisscross the region. Panama Rocks Park has a large ridge of quartz running through it. Some believe that quartz deposits of this nature are spiritual vortexes, such as Skellig Michael in County Kerry, Ireland. Perhaps ley lines and quartz vortexes attracted spiritual people to this region over the years. Certainly, many movements have started here, drawing people for decades to learn and share their arts and talents and to enlighten their spiritual lives.

The Chautauqua movement began here, and many spiritualists call Lily Dale their home. Quakers, Amish and Mormons have left their marks, as have more mainstream faiths. The national basilica for Our Lady of Fatima is located in Lewiston, and Father Baker built Our Lady of Victory Basilica by asking Catholics worldwide to send just twenty-five cents each to help with costs.

Many new movements were developed with the idea of creating utopian societies, including several communities throughout New York State such as Oneida, Seneca Falls (birthplace of the women's rights movement), Skaneateles and Mordecai Noah's failed attempts at an Ararat on Grand Island.

THE BURNED-OVER DISTRICT

The whole of Western and Central New York is often referred to as the "burned-over district" when discussing religious movements of the 1800s. The term was coined by Charles Grandison Finney during "America's Second Grand Awakening." Finney migrated to the region with his family, becoming a lawyer, and at age twenty-nine he "saw the light." Forming an evangelical style of Presbyterianism using what he called the "New Measures," Finney was one of many traveling tent preachers of the era.

At the height of the religious movements in the region, many evangelists shied away from Western New York, saying it had become oversaturated. Few would listen to anything outside of their own views, making conversion impossible.

THE CHAUTAUQUA MOVEMENT

Opened in 1874 as the Chautauqua Lake Sunday School Assembly, Chautauqua Institution is known worldwide for its summer lecture series. A Methodist minister, John Heyl Vincent, partnered with an Ohio philanthropic businessman, Lewis Miller. They created a place for Sunday school teachers to learn and share. What they started became a movement that continued to grow nationally throughout the late nineteenth to early twentieth centuries.

Independent Chautauquas emerged at other beautiful sites, usually semirural and close to transportation such as railways. Beginning in Western New York, at the height of the movement there were hundreds of these locations throughout the country.

In 1904, a new form of Chautauqua gained popularity—the Circuit Chautauqua. These assemblies moved about, much like the popular circuses of the era. Chautauqua tents would appear outside a town, and then in a few days they would move on. Rather than travel with a particular tent, performers and lecturers moved from location to location in daily cycles as part of a series. These Circuit Chautauquas lost their appeal by the 1940s, but in their time they visited over ten thousand communities.

From the beginning, Chautauqua was nondenominational. While it began for the purpose of religious study, it quickly took on a life of its own, continuing today to include its ever popular lecture series, as well as music, performance, teaching, preaching and recreation.

The Chautauqua Institution on Chautauqua Lake in Western New York is a gated community with its own fire department, police department, library and post office. More than 2,000 permanent residents call it home, with over 100,000 visitors attending events each summer. It is so beautiful that some people go there just to picnic by the lake and enjoy the institution's spirit.

Lily Dale

Spiritualism gained popularity in the 1800s. By 1897, there were millions of followers both in the United States and Europe. Basic spiritualist belief is that man is both physical and spiritual, encompassing God, seeking truth, living responsibly and having continuity in life. Spiritualists supported the abolition of slavery and women's suffrage.

The Lily Dale Assembly, a spiritualist community located on the shore of Cassadaga Lake, was established in 1879. It is the largest center for spiritualist development in the world. The wooded community is home to many mediums, teachers and healers. Like Chautauqua, Lily Dale is

Pet cemetery, Lily Dale. *Courtesy of the author.*

internationally known for its lectures and workshops. Healing sessions are held on site at the spiritualist church.

The Lily Dale Assembly began in 1844 with a series of lectures in Laona, New York, which led to the formation of a spiritualist group in Laona. Interest continued in the 1870s, when Dr. Jeremiah Carter was moved by spirit voices to establish a camp at Cassadaga. He ignored the calling, but as the voices became more insistent, he did as they beckoned. This brought him to the lakeside home of Willard Alden.

Alden had taken an interest in Spiritualism. A grove on his property became the site of many gatherings. When Carter told Alden of the voices, he agreed that the grove would be donated for a camp meeting, and a committee was formed. By 1879, they had raised enough funds to build several cottages. The Alden property became Lily Dale, and the beautiful Alden farmhouse is now the community's Leolyn Hotel.

Perhaps the most peaceful and heartwarming location in Lily Dale is the pet cemetery. Here, pets are laid to rest among the trees, with headstones testifying to the love they were given in life and the love they still have. A visitor will soon notice that cats can be found in great number throughout the community, on porches, under bushes, in trees and in windows.

QUAKERS AND SHAKERS

The Quakers and the Amish have both played roles in the history of Western New York. After the American Revolution, many Quakers migrated west from the Hudson Valley to settle first in Ontario, Canada, in 1789. Western New York settlement took place as these Quakers moved through New York on their way to Canada. Eventually, the Friends also came from Pennsylvania and New Jersey. During this early period, Quakers typically settled in Hamburg, Orchard Park, Boston and Buffalo. Active in the antislavery movement, the Quakers risked their own reputations and lives on the Underground Railroad.

The Shaker movement, or the United Society for Believers in Christ's Second Appearing, began in 1758 with Ann Lee. James and Jane Wardley, who had been Quakers, were inspired one day by the "Spirit" and began to dance wildly. This led to the nickname "Shaking Quakers," or Shakers. When "Mother" Lee joined their small assembly, she had a revelation that said she was the female counterpart to Christ, which led to persecution in Europe and migration to America in the 1770s.

Moving to the frontier made perfect sense for the Shakers, who were also persecuted in New England. By 1840, the movement had grown to six thousand in twenty communities. When New York State used the law of eminent domain to take the land for its plans of a canal in 1836, the last larger settlement at Sodus Bay on Lake Ontario was moved to Groveland in the Western New York southern tier. One building of this Groveland community can still be seen just off Route 36, outside Mount Morris. Additionally, three buildings were incorporated into the nearby Groveland Correctional Institute. Another building was relocated to Genesee Country Village in Mumford.

THE AMISH

The Amish split from the old Mennonite faith in 1693, when a group of Mennonites led by Jacob Amman felt that the church was losing its purity. They first appear in America in the 1700s.

When we think of the Amish, we usually associate them with the state of Pennsylvania, but they also have a presence in the Western New York southern tier. For example, the population of the town of Leon in Cattaraugus County is more than half Amish, with their handiwork and craftsmanship gracing its shops. Williamsville, a suburb of Buffalo, is the location of a beautiful example of Mennonite architecture, the Mennonite Meeting House. Lovely in its simplicity, nestled among twentieth-century shops on Main Street, it is a stone structure built in 1834. The local limestone used for this building encases many fossils from the ancient seabed of this region.

Amid all of the gadgetry, hustle and bustle of modern life, one may still travel the roadways of our southern tier to enjoy the slower pace set by horse-drawn buggies driven by men in black hats and ladies in bonnets.

MORMONS AND LAKE TONAWANDA

Known as the father of the Mormon movement, or Latter Day Saints, Vermont-born Joseph Smith took up residence in Western New York. It was his belief that an angel gave him the plates for the Mormon Bible. These were found on a hillside near Palmyra, New York. This book told of the migration of Nephites and Lamanites to America. Smith became a prophet for the chosen people who would build the Kingdom of God on earth. Many poor farmers and craftsman were attracted to the hopeful religion, as it offered them stability.

Smith introduced the idea of polygamy. After taking another wife (kidnapped Mason William Morgan's widow), he and his followers migrated farther west to Ohio. Joseph Smith was murdered in 1844, but the controversial movement continued to grow. The largest group of Mormons eventually landed in Salt Lake City, Utah, under the leadership of Brigham Young.

Lake Tonawanda is sacred to the Mormons. A prehistoric body of water created over ten thousand years ago during the last ice age, it was located on the upper Niagara escarpment. Lake Tonawanda was fed by Lake Erie and drained in Lake Ontario via multiple waterfalls. These falls outlets were located at Holly, Medina, Gasport, Lockport and Lewiston. The falls at Lewiston was the main spillway, birthplace of Niagara Falls.

As it was shallow, when Lake Erie's water level dropped, Lake Tonawanda evaporated, reminding one of the turloughs or disappearing lakes of Ireland. The only difference is that the turloughs return after a rain. Then again, we might think of it as a turlough, since Tonawanda floods during heavy rains,

Joseph Smith, Mormon founder.
*Courtesy of the Library of Congress
Prints and Photographs Division.*

with homes and roads along Tonawanda Creek continuing to sink in the unstable soil of this ancient lake bed.

At one time, Tonawanda Lake covered most of Western New York to Rochester. The Mormons considered this lake to be part of the sacred homeland described in the Book of Mormon; indeed, the correlations are astounding. This also explains why Mordecai Noah considered Grand Island significant. The island was once at the bottom of the lake. For the Mormons, Lake Tonawanda was "the inland sea," or the sea that divided the land in their mythology.

The comparisons between the Book of Mormon and local ancient geography are complicated. The book describes a land of waters (the Great Lakes, Finger Lakes, streams, rivers, ponds and creeks); a land to the north that can foster life (Canada); highlands in the south (Allegany Plateau), with its forests and plentiful game; and down the middle, the Batavia Moraine (a dry neck of land for travel).

The waters of Lake Erie and the Niagara River again played a significant role in the history of Western New York.

Father Baker and Our Lady of Fatima Shrine

While neither Father Baker nor the Shrine at Lewiston can be considered movements, they have definitely left an indelible mark on the region.

Nelson Henry Baker was born in Lackawanna, New York, in 1842 to a German Lutheran father and an Irish Catholic mother. He converted to Catholicism in 1851, fought in the American Civil War, including Gettysburg, and returned home to become a successful businessman. After a summer cruise on Lake Erie in 1869, Nelson decided to become a priest and entered Our Lady of Angels Seminary, now Niagara University. Nelson's devotions took him to Rome and Paris, where he acquired his lifelong devotion to Our Lady of Victory. In his lifetime, Nelson experienced the life of a mixed-marriage family, fought in our country's bloodiest war and had been an entrepreneur. He truly understood the common man, and in 1881, he was placed in charge of three Limestone Hill facilities: St. Patrick's Church, St. Joseph's Orphanage and St. John's Protectory. They were in dire financial straits, with debts in today's terms of over $1 million. He used all of his own money, in addition to writing letters nationwide to Catholic women asking them to join the Association of Our Lady of Victory. Monies raised paid the debts for these organizations. Natural gas wells on the lands also helped offset costs.

Father Baker was appalled by the deaths of many poor and orphaned children. Our Lady of Victory Infant Home became a major project for him. In 1916, the previous orphanage was severely damaged by fire, and Father Baker's idea for a maternity hospital was squelched by new nursing regulations. At a meeting following the fire, the priest told parishioners that rather than be defeated by the turn of events, he would build a great cathedral. Of course, they were surprised, especially since no money had been set aside for such a huge undertaking. But they broke ground for the cathedral and a new school as well.

Penniless, Monsignor Baker, the Padre of the Poor, died at age ninety-four. People lined up for hours to say farewell. Today, his legacy lives on in Our Lady of Victory Basilica, Victory Services and in Father Baker's school and children's home. In 1987, the Vatican bestowed him with the title "Servant of God," which began his canonization to sainthood. Today, Monsignor Baker is interred beneath the basilica. His Association of the Lady of Victory now includes over seventy thousand people worldwide.

The sculpture of Father Baker with an angel and children atop Our Lady of Victory Basilica. *Courtesy of the author.*

Not yet a saint according to church law, Father Nelson Baker became the people's saint a long time ago. The sculptures of angels surrounded by children that cap the entranceway to the basilica give testimony to that.

Less impressive in stature, Our Lady of Fatima Shrine in Lewiston sits atop the escarpment overlooking the town of Lewiston. More contemporary in its design, the main dome is a world globe capped by a statue of Our Lady. This national basilica and holy shrine to the lady is operated by the Barnabites, the first order named for the Apostle Paul.

ELBERT HUBBARD AND THE ROYCROFTERS

Although the story of Elbert Hubbard is not one of religion, the legacy of his Roycroft movement is still felt today. Born in Illinois, Hubbard came to Buffalo to work for the Larkin Soap Company. He is best remembered for the Roycroft trademark. This was part of the arts and crafts movement of the late 1800s, and the Roycrofters could be found in their shops or on the porch of the Roycroft Inn in East Aurora, discussing wit, news of the day, politics, humanities and the arts. They were leading producers of Mission-style products, with its focus on handmade wares featuring natural materials.

Hubbard published two magazines, the *Philistine* and the *Fra*. He was a thinker, lecturer and author of "A Message to Garcia," an essay about duty based on the Spanish-American War.

On May 1, 1915, Elbert Hubbard and his wife boarded the *Lusitania* in New York City. Hubbard was on his way to Europe to act as a peace advocate but never reached his destination. Tragically, he became a casualty of the very war he wished to end when the ship was torpedoed and sunk.

The memory of Elbert Hubbard and the legacy of the Roycrofters lives on at the Roycroft Inn in East Aurora.

THEY WERE HERE

A Conclusion

From the most ancient times of glaciers and Mound Builders to the Cat People and pioneers, from war time to peace and boom time to present day, Western New York has held a mystique for the explorer, adventurer and artist. Something here inspires.

Buffalo is famous for more than wings, great inventions and innovations; it is known for its architecture, arts and sports. Frank Lloyd Wright built here, as did Louis Sullivan, Henry Hobson Richardson and many more. Western New York inspired movements from Chautauqua to Lily Dale and the Roycrofters. There have been great men and women, such as Father Baker, Tim Russert, Jack Kemp (politician and former Buffalo Bill) and Mary Jemison, "the White Woman of the Genesee," not to mention two presidents of the United States.

World-famous planners built this region, such as surveyor Joseph Ellicott and landscaper Frederick Law Olmsted. During the hard times of the Great Depression, the Civilian Conservation Corps and Works Progress Administration built parks and bridges and started the Buffalo Philharmonic here. Were it not for the Pan-American Exposition, much of the Delaware Park and Parkside District would not be as it is, with the Albright Knox and Buffalo-Erie County Historical Society as centerpieces.

We are rich in cultural history, with musicians, stars of the stage, writers, composers, painters and sculptors such as Larry Griffis, who gave us Griffis Park in Ashford Hollow.

And we cannot forget them as we wander the park-like setting of Forest Lawn Cemetery, where they call to us from the past: the great Seneca chief

Red Jacket; moguls and businessmen such as Birge (wallpaper), William Fargo (Wells Fargo), Larkin (soap and Buffalo Pottery Co.) and dentist Alfred Southwick (inventor of the electric chair); President Millard Fillmore; and activist Mary Talbert. They keep urging us forward, asking us to continue their legacies.

There are other past enterprises, too: the Bell Company of Boston, New York, largest manufacturer of cow and sheep bells in the United States, and the Kazoo Factory in Eden, the only maker of metal kazoos in North America today. Anne Bunis started the Sample Dress Shop in her home on Hertel Avenue in 1929, and it grew into a major Western New York chain. When we felt blue, we might have ridden the hand-carved ponies at the Herschell Carrousel Factory in North Tonawanda or visited Earl's Diner in Chaffee for some spirit-warming good food and country music.

Western New York was built on the backs and spirits of many great people. We must remember our patriots, not only those great men and women of the early wars who settled this frontier but also those of later wars. Not all can be mentioned here, but one who must be recalled is Matt Urban.

Born in Buffalo on August 25, 1919, as Matty Louis Unbanowski, Matt Urban is considered the most combat-decorated soldier in the country. Known by German foes as the "Ghost" because he repeatedly returned to fight even when seriously wounded, Matt Urban was a World War II hero. He was awarded seven Purple Hearts, the Legion Merit, the Croix de Guerre with a Silver Star and the Congressional Medal of Honor. All in all, he held twenty-nine American, French and Belgian decorations.

Matt Urban was a courageous man, a natural leader and a Western New Yorker to the core. His deeds say everything about the people who live here.

Last but not least, one of the most lasting influences on American patriotism is the work of Mount Morris native Francis Bellamy. His story is the most fitting to end this book; it is a story about a former wilderness forest area that became a bustling industrial giant and a place of "Good Neighbors."

Francis Bellamy, the son of a Baptist minister, was born on May 18, 1855. Educated in Rome and later at the University of Rochester, Francis studied to become a Baptist minister like his father. After his graduation, he took a position as a minister in Little Falls, New York. In 1892, a children's magazine, the *Youth's Companion*, contracted with Bellamy to write a pledge.

The Francis Bellamy Home, Mt. Morris, New York. *Courtesy of the author.*

It was the very pledge that every schoolchild in America knows by heart, recited for over one hundred years by young and old alike: "The Pledge of Allegiance."

Slightly different in its original form, the pledge read as follows: "I Pledge Allegiance to my Flag and the Republic for which it stands, one nation indivisible with liberty and justice for all."

The word "to" was added in October of the same year to make it read "to the Republic." In 1924, "my Flag" was changed to "the Flag." It was not until 1954 that "under God" was added.

Francis Bellamy, minister and writer, died on August 28, 1931. He is buried in the Rome, New York cemetery. A marker on Route 36 shows the site of his childhood home in Mount Morris. Of all the Western New Yorkers who have influenced its residents, their country and the world, Francis Bellamy's contribution is one we cannot forget:

They Were Here

I pledge allegiance to the Flag of the United States of America,
and to the Republic for which it stands: one Nation, under God,
indivisible,
With Liberty and Justice for all.

The pleasure of living and working in Western New York is something we sometimes take for granted, but when residents move away, they often come back. They remember home as it was and as it is. They carry the power of the river and the falls, holding on to the staunch hardiness of the first settlers to come here, knowing that what these settlers accomplished has made us who we are.

SELECTED BIBLIOGRAPHY

Cross, Whitney R. *The Burned-Over District: The Social and Intellectual History of Enthusiastic Religion in Western New York, 1800–1850.* Ithaca, NY: Cornell University Press, 2006.

Goldman, Mark. *City on the Edge.* Amherst, NY: Prometheus Books, 2007.

Headrick, Maggie, and Celia Ehrlich. *Seeing Buffalo.* Buffalo, NY: Headrick & Ehrlich, 1978.

Klees, Emerson. *Underground Railroad Tales: With Route Through the Finger Lakes Region.* Rochester, NY: Friends of the Finger Lakes Publishing,1997.

Leon, Paul. *Chautauqua Ghosts.* Westfield, NY: Chautauqua Region Press, 1996.

Morganstein, Martin, and Joan L. Cregg. *Images of America: Erie Canal.* Portsmouth, NH: Arcadia, 2001.

Parker, Arthur C. *Skunny Wundy: Seneca Indian Tales.* Syracuse, NY: Syracuse University Press, 1994.

Rapp, Marvin A. *Canal Water and Whiskey.* Buffalo, NY: Heritage Press, 1992.

Wilder, Patrick. *Seaway Trail Guidebook to the War of 1812.* Oswego, NY: Seaway Trail, Inc., 1987.

Winfield, Mason. *Haunted Places of Western New York: A Supernatural Tour Guide.* Buffalo, NY: Western New York Wares, 2003.

INTERNET RESOURCES

Buffalonet. www.buffalonet.org.
Buffalonian. www.buffalonian.com.
Forest Lawn Cemetery. www.forest-lawn.com/?select=news.

ABOUT THE AUTHOR

Storyteller, author and educator Lorna MacDonald Czarnota has delighted audiences in schools, libraries, festivals and conferences throughout the United States, Canada and Ireland with traditional and original stories since 1985. Her work features historical presentations, including those on the American Civil War, the Middle Ages, the Dust Bowl and colonial America. She is a vocalist with the Blue Eagle String Band, presenting music of the Great Depression.

Lorna's programs include storytelling, writing workshops and motivational presentations. She specializes in work with at-risk youth, therapeutic narrative, Celtic folklore and the use of music and song to enhance story. Her writing and recording accomplishments include *Medieval Tales that Kids Can Read and Tell*; "The Bleeding Heart"; *The Healing Heart Communities*; "One Lace Glove"; *August House Book of Scary Stories*; *Crossroads: Stories of Choice and Empowerment*; and *Dancing in Dark Waters*.

Lorna is a recipient of the 2006 Oracle Award from the National Storytelling Network, the Hopevale Incorporated Volunteer of the Year Award and the Storytelling World Award and was nominated as a Univera, United Way Community Hero. Visit her website at www.storyhavenstudio.com.

IF YOU ENJOYED THIS BOOK, YOU MAY ALSO ENJOY:

Forgotten Tales of New York
Melanie Zimmer
ISBN 978-1-59629-678-7
$14.99 • 144 pages • 5 x 7 • 17 images

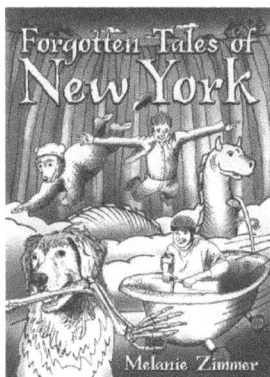

Few New Yorkers remember the night when firemen, in tuxedos and top hats, were dragged from a ball to extinguish a Waterloo blaze, or the typographical error that reported Theodore Roosevelt taking a "bath" instead of his presidential "oath." Still fewer remember Cephas Bennett, a missionary from Utica and printer of the first Burmese Bible, or H.L. Mencken's humorous article on the history of the bathtub, still quoted today as factual although entirely invented. Seasoned storyteller Melanie Zimmer seamlessly weaves together these hard-to-believe, yet entirely true, tales. From the monster of Seneca Lake to the man who inspired the American icon Uncle Sam, discover the lost secrets of the Empire State.

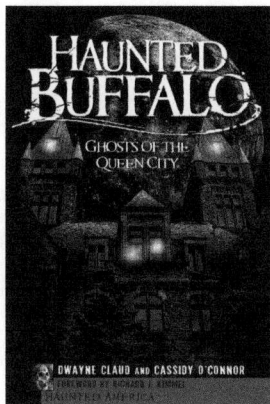

Haunted Buffalo: Ghosts of the Queen City
Dwayne Claud and Cassidy O'Connor
ISBN 978-1-59629-775-3
$19.99 • 128 pages • 6 x 9 • Over 30 images

Grab pen and paper, a flashlight and a camera and prepare to embark on the haunted adventure of a lifetime using this comprehensive guide to some of Buffalo's spookiest sites. Avid ghost hunter and paranormal investigator Dwayne Claud and researcher Cassidy O'Connor entertain readers with stories of the city's most acclaimed spooks and spirits, such as Tanya, the five-year-old who can be spotted bouncing on guest beds at the Grand Island Holiday Inn. The book includes twisted tales from the Buffalo Psychiatric Center, as well as stories of roaming spirits at Frontier House—a hotel frequented by figures such as Mark Twain and President McKinley. This gripping collection of ghostly tales is sure to thrill anyone fascinated by the unknown

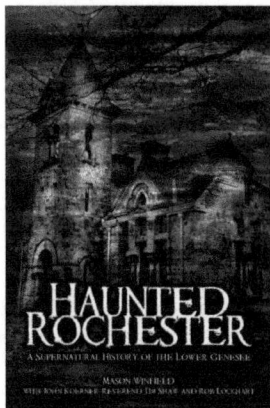

Haunted Rochester: A Supernatural History of the Lower Genesee

Mason Winfield, John Koerner, Reverend Tim Shaw & Rob Lockhart
ISBN 978-1-59629-418-9
$19.99 • 128 pages • 6 x 9 • 6 images

Supernatural historian Winfield and the research team from Haunted History Ghost Walks, Inc., lead a spiritual safari through the Seneca homeland of the "Sweet River Valley" and the modern city in its place. After their survey of Rochester's haunted history and tradition, "the Flour City" will never look the same.

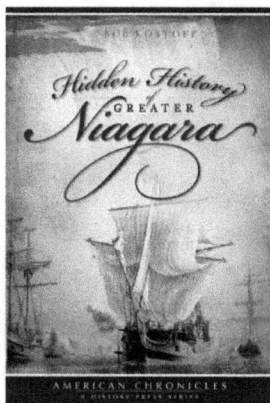

Hidden History of Greater Niagara

Bob Kostoff
ISBN 978-1-59629-789-0
$19.99 • 128 pages • 6 x 9 • Over 25 images

Niagara Falls is known as a scenic honeymoon destination and a standing challenge for any daredevil with a barrel, but Kostoff proves that from illegal women's boxing matches on the North Tonawanda water to hangings morphing into musical celebrations, there's much more to this storied land than its familiar enchantments.

Visit us at
www.historypress.net